INVESTING IN MUTUAL FUNDS 101

A BEGINNER'S GUIDE TO BUILDING WEALTH THROUGH SMART INVESTING

Usiere Uko

ISBN-13: 979-8-388-92753-8

FIRST EDITION

...To new frontiers, learning and growing

CONTENTS

INTRODUCTION

I nvesting in mutual funds is an excellent way to build wealth over the long term, especially for beginner investors. Mutual funds offer a simple, cost-effective way to diversify your portfolio across multiple asset classes and investment styles.

By investing in mutual funds, you have the opportunity to participate in the growth of financial instruments you may not be able to afford to invest in individually.

However, with so many mutual funds available, it can be challenging to navigate the complex world of investing.

In this book, we will cover the basics of mutual fund investing, including how mutual funds work, the benefits and risks of investing in mutual funds, different types of mutual funds available, and how to choose the right mutual funds for your investment goals.

We will also provide essential information on how to analyze mutual fund performance, minimize your tax liability, and avoid common investor mistakes.

Whether you are a novice investor just starting your investment journey or a seasoned investor looking to expand your portfolio, this book will provide you with the knowledge and tools to make informed investment decisions and build wealth through smart investing in mutual funds.

1: INTRODUCTION TO MUTUAL FUNDS
UNDERSTANDING THE BASICS

Investing in mutual funds is one of the easiest ways for beginners to get started with investing. A mutual fund is a type of investment vehicle that pools money from multiple investors to buy a diversified portfolio of stocks, bonds, or other securities.

The mutual fund is managed by a professional portfolio manager, who makes investment decisions on behalf of the investors.

Mutual funds have become increasingly popular over the years because of their ease of use, low cost, and diversification benefits. They offer a convenient way for investors to gain exposure to a variety of asset classes, sectors, and regions, without the need for extensive research or active management.

In this chapter, we will explore the basics of mutual funds and their key features.

WHAT IS A MUTUAL FUND?

A mutual fund is a type of investment company that pools money from investors to buy a diversified portfolio of securities. Investors buy shares in the mutual fund, and the value of those shares is determined by the performance of the underlying securities.

TYPES OF MUTUAL FUNDS

There are many types of mutual funds available, including equity funds, bond funds, index funds, sector funds, and international funds.

Each type of mutual fund has its own investment objective and strategy.

BENEFITS OF INVESTING IN MUTUAL FUNDS

Mutual funds offer several benefits to investors, including diversification, professional management, and low cost. They are also easy to buy and sell, and provide investors with access to a wide range of asset classes.

RISKS OF INVESTING IN MUTUAL FUNDS

Like all investments, mutual funds carry risks. The value of the mutual fund can go up or down depending on the performance of the underlying securities. Investors may also be subject to fees and taxes.

CHOOSING A MUTUAL FUND

Choosing a mutual fund requires careful consideration of several factors, including the investment objective, performance history, and fees. Investors should also consider their own risk tolerance and investment goals.

Mutual funds offer a convenient and accessible way for investors to gain exposure to a diversified portfolio of securities.

They offer several benefits, including diversification, professional management, and low cost.

2: BENEFITS OF INVESTING IN MUTUAL FUNDS

Mutual funds are a popular investment option for many investors. They offer several benefits that make them an attractive investment vehicle. In this chapter, we will explore the benefits of investing in mutual funds.

1. DIVERSIFICATION

One of the main benefits of investing in mutual funds is diversification. Mutual funds invest in a variety of stocks, bonds, and other securities, which helps to spread out the risk.

By investing in a diversified portfolio of securities, investors can reduce their overall risk and potentially earn higher returns.

2. PROFESSIONAL MANAGEMENT

Another benefit of investing in mutual funds is professional management. Mutual funds are managed by professional portfolio managers who have expertise in selecting and managing a portfolio of securities.

These portfolio managers have access to research, resources, and market data that individual investors may not have. This can help to improve the performance of the mutual fund and potentially increase returns.

3. LOW COST

Mutual funds are generally low-cost investments. They have lower fees than many other types of investments, such as individual stocks or bonds. This is because the costs of managing a mutual fund are spread across a large number of investors. Additionally, some mutual funds have lower fees than others, which means that investors can choose a mutual fund that fits their budget.

4. CONVENIENCE AND ACCESSIBILITY

Mutual funds are easy to buy and sell. They are available through brokerage firms, financial advisors, and directly from the mutual fund company. This makes them a convenient and accessible investment option for many investors.

5. ACCESS TO A WIDE RANGE OF ASSET CLASSES

Mutual funds provide investors with access to a wide range of asset classes, including stocks, bonds, and alternative investments. This allows investors to diversify their portfolio and potentially earn higher returns.

6. LIQUIDITY

Mutual funds are a liquid investment, which means that investors can buy and sell shares at any time. This makes them a good option for investors who may need to access their money quickly.

Investing in mutual funds offers several benefits to investors. Mutual funds provide diversification, professional management, low cost, convenience and accessibility, access to a wide range of asset classes, and liquidity.

However, you should carefully consider the risks and choose

mutual funds based on your investment objectives and risk tolerance.

In the next chapter, we will discuss in detail the types of mutual funds.

3: EQUITY FUNDS

Equity funds, also known as stock funds, are mutual funds that invest primarily in stocks or equities. These funds are popular among investors who are looking for long-term growth and are willing to take on more risk for potentially higher returns.

Equity funds can invest in a variety of stocks, including large-cap, mid-cap, small-cap, and international stocks.

TYPES OF EQUITY FUNDS

1. LARGE-CAP EQUITY FUNDS:

Large-cap equity funds are mutual funds that invest primarily in large-cap stocks, which are companies with a market capitalization of $10 billion or more.

These funds aim to provide long-term capital appreciation by investing in companies that are well-established, financially stable, and have a strong market position.

Investing in large-cap equity funds can be a good choice for investors who seek exposure to blue-chip companies with a long history of stable earnings and dividend payments. These funds are generally considered to be less risky than small-cap or mid-cap funds, as large-cap companies are often more resilient during economic downturns.

Some large-cap equity funds invest only in companies located within a specific geographic region, such as the United States or Asia, while others invest globally. Some funds may also have a specific investment style, such as value or growth.

Value funds invest in companies that are undervalued by the market and have a potential for growth, while growth funds invest in companies with strong growth potential, regardless of their current market valuation.

While large-cap equity funds can provide solid long-term returns, investors should keep in mind that they are subject to market risk and fluctuations. In addition, investors should evaluate the expense ratio and other fees associated with the fund, as these costs can erode the returns. It is important to research the fund's investment objectives, performance history, and fees before investing.

2. MID-CAP EQUITY FUNDS

Mid-cap equity funds are mutual funds that invest primarily in stocks of mid-sized companies, which are typically companies with market capitalizations between $2 billion and $10 billion.

Mid-cap companies are generally less established than large-cap companies but have more growth potential than small-cap companies. Mid-cap equity funds can be a good choice for investors who are looking for the potential for higher returns than large-cap equity funds but are willing to accept slightly more risk.

The companies in which mid-cap equity funds invest are generally considered to be more stable than small-cap companies, but they can also offer more growth potential than large-cap companies. These companies often have established track records, solid earnings growth, and a proven business model, which can make them attractive investment options.

Investors in mid-cap equity funds should be aware that these funds can be more volatile than large-cap equity funds, meaning that the value of the fund can fluctuate more rapidly in response to market conditions. However, the potential for higher returns may make them a good choice for investors who are willing to accept a moderate level of risk.

Like large-cap equity funds, mid-cap equity funds can be actively managed or passively managed. Actively managed funds are managed by investment professionals who actively select the stocks in the fund's portfolio based on their analysis and research. Passively managed funds, on the other hand, seek to track the performance of a specific index, such as the S&P MidCap 400 Index.

Overall, mid-cap equity funds can be a good choice for investors who are looking for a balance between risk and potential returns. By diversifying their portfolio with mid-cap equity funds, investors can gain exposure to a diverse range of mid-sized companies that have the potential to provide strong long-term returns.

3. SMALL-CAP EQUITY FUNDS

Small-cap equity funds are mutual funds that invest in the stocks of companies with small market capitalizations. Market capitalization refers to the total value of a company's outstanding shares of stock, and small-cap companies typically have a market capitalization between $300 million and $2 billion.

Small-cap equity funds are often considered riskier than large-cap equity funds because smaller companies may have less stable financials and may be more susceptible to economic downturns. However, they also have the potential to provide higher returns than larger companies because they have more room for growth.

Small-cap equity funds are typically more volatile than large-cap equity funds, and their performance can fluctuate widely.

Therefore, they are generally recommended for investors with a high tolerance for risk who are willing to accept the potential for high returns in exchange for higher volatility.

Investors who are interested in small-cap equity funds should research the individual fund's investment strategy and holdings, as well as the fund manager's track record. It is also important to consider the fees associated with investing in the fund, including expense ratios and any front-end or back-end loads.

4. INTERNATIONAL EQUITY FUNDS

International equity funds are mutual funds that invest in stocks of companies outside the investor's home country. These funds provide exposure to companies located in foreign countries, including both developed and emerging markets.

Investing in international equity funds can provide diversification benefits to investors' portfolios, as they offer exposure to different regions, industries, and currencies. It can also provide opportunities for higher returns and lower correlation with domestic markets. However, investing in international equity funds also comes with risks, including currency fluctuations, political instability, and differences in accounting and regulatory practices.

There are different types of international equity funds, including regional funds that focus on specific regions such as Europe, Asia, or Latin America, and global funds that invest in companies across the world. Emerging market funds are another type of international equity fund that focus on companies in developing countries with higher growth potential but also higher risk.

Investors should carefully consider their investment goals, risk tolerance, and time horizon before investing in international equity funds. They should also research the fund's investment strategy, fees, and track record to ensure they are making an informed decision. Working with a financial advisor can also help investors navigate the complexities of international investing and build a well-diversified portfolio.

ADVANTAGES OF EQUITY FUNDS:

1. **Diversification:** Equity funds provide diversification by investing in a portfolio of stocks across different sectors and industries.

2. **Professional Management:** Equity funds are managed by professional fund managers who have experience in stock market investing and can make investment decisions on behalf of investors.

3. **Liquidity:** Equity funds are highly liquid and can be bought and sold easily, making them a good choice for investors who need access to their money quickly.

4. **Potential for High Returns:** Equity funds have the potential for high returns over the long term, making them a good choice for investors who are willing to take on more risk for potentially higher returns.

DISADVANTAGES OF EQUITY FUNDS

1. **Higher Risk:** Equity funds are more volatile than bond funds and have a higher risk of loss.

2. **Fees:** Equity funds charge management fees, which can eat into investment returns over time. It is important for investors to consider these fees when selecting an equity fund.

3. **Market Fluctuations:** The stock market can be volatile and unpredictable, which can lead to fluctuations in the value of equity funds. This can be concerning for investors who are not comfortable with market volatility or who have a shorter investment time horizon.

4. **Potential for Underperformance:** While equity funds have

the potential for high returns, they also have the potential to underperform their benchmark or other investment options. This can be due to factors such as poor fund management or unfavorable market conditions.

TIPS FOR INVESTING IN EQUITY FUNDS

1. Consider your investment goals and risk tolerance before selecting an equity fund.

2. Do your research on the fund's performance history, management team, and fees before investing.

3. Diversify your portfolio by investing in a mix of large-cap, mid-cap, small-cap, and international equity funds.

4. Regularly review your portfolio to ensure it aligns with your investment goals and make any necessary adjustments over time.

5. Be patient and focus on the long-term potential of equity funds, rather than short-term market fluctuations.

EXAMPLES AND CASE STUDIES

S&P 500 INDEX FUND

One of the most popular equity funds is the S&P 500 Index Fund. This fund tracks the performance of the S&P 500 index, which is made up of 500 of the largest companies in the US.

By investing in this fund, investors can gain exposure to a broad range of industries and companies within the US market. For example, the Vanguard 500 Index Fund is one of the largest S&P 500 index funds, with over $1 trillion in assets under management.

SMALL-CAP EQUITY FUND

Another type of equity fund is a small-cap equity fund, which invests in small-cap companies. These companies are typically those with a market capitalization of between $300 million and $2 billion. These companies have the potential for high growth, but also carry a higher level of risk.

An example of a small-cap equity fund is the T. Rowe Price Small-Cap Fund, which has consistently outperformed its benchmark over the long term.

GROWTH VS. VALUE FUNDS

One of the key decisions that investors must make when investing in equity funds is whether to invest in growth or value funds.

Growth funds invest in companies that are expected to grow at a faster rate than the overall market, while value funds invest in companies that are undervalued by the market. Let's take a look at a case study to see the performance difference between these two types of funds.

Between 2000 and 2010, growth funds significantly outperformed value funds. For example, the Vanguard Growth Index Fund returned an average of 1.36% per year, while the Vanguard Value Index Fund returned an average of 0.14% per year over this period.

However, in the following decade, value funds outperformed growth funds. From 2010 to 2020, the Vanguard Value Index Fund returned an average of 9.1% per year, while the Vanguard Growth Index Fund returned an average of 7.3% per year.

This case study highlights the importance of diversification and considering different market cycles when investing in equity funds.

Equity funds can be a valuable investment option if you are seeking long-term growth and are willing to take on more risk. It is important to carefully consider the advantages and disadvantages of equity funds and to do your research before investing to ensure you select the best option for your investment goals and risk tolerance.

By diversifying your portfolio and regularly reviewing your investments, you can potentially maximize the benefits of equity funds over time.

4: DEBT FUNDS

Debt funds, also known as fixed-income funds, are mutual funds that invest primarily in fixed-income securities such as bonds, treasury bills, and commercial papers. These funds are popular among investors who are looking for a steady stream of income and are willing to accept lower returns for lower risk.

Debt funds can invest in a variety of fixed-income securities, including government bonds, corporate bonds, and municipal bonds.

TYPES OF DEBT FUNDS

1. GOVERNMENT BOND FUNDS

Government bond funds are a type of debt fund that invests in bonds issued by the government, typically of a particular country. These funds invest in fixed-income securities that are issued and backed by the government, making them relatively low-risk investments.

The income generated by these bonds is often in the form of regular interest payments, and the principal is returned when the bonds mature.

Government bond funds can be further categorized based on the duration of the bonds they hold. For instance, short-term government bond funds invest in bonds that mature in three years or less, while long-term government bond funds invest in bonds that mature in ten years or more.

These types of funds can be suitable if you desire a steady stream of income and a low-risk investment option. Additionally, they can be an excellent option for diversifying your portfolio beyond equities and other high-risk investments.

2. CORPORATE BOND FUNDS

Corporate bond funds are a type of debt mutual fund that invests in a diversified portfolio of fixed-income securities issued by corporations. These funds primarily invest in bonds issued by companies of different sizes, industries, and credit ratings.

Corporate bond funds offers a higher yield than government bond funds as corporate bonds typically carry a higher credit risk. However, this higher yield also comes with an increased risk of default. Corporate bond funds are categorized based on the credit quality of the bonds they invest in.

For instance, investment-grade corporate bond funds invest in high-quality bonds issued by companies with good credit ratings.

On the other hand, high-yield corporate bond funds, also known as junk bond funds, invest in lower-rated bonds issued by companies with a higher risk of default.

Corporate bond funds are suitable for investors looking for steady income streams from their investments, particularly those with a low tolerance for risk. They are a good option for those who want to diversify their portfolios beyond government bonds and savings accounts.

However, it is essential to note that corporate bond funds are not risk-free, and there is always a chance that a company may default on its bonds, resulting in losses for investors. As such, you should carefully research and evaluate the credit quality of the bonds in the fund's portfolio before investing.

3. MUNICIPAL BOND FUNDS

Municipal bond funds are another type of debt fund that invests in bonds issued by state and local governments, as well as agencies and municipalities. These bonds are used to finance public projects such as schools, hospitals, highways, and other infrastructure projects.

Municipal bond funds can provide tax advantages for investors since the interest income from these bonds is typically exempt from federal income taxes and, in some cases, state and local taxes.

However, the tax-exempt status of municipal bonds depends on the specific bonds and your tax situation.

Like other debt funds, municipal bond funds also carry credit risk, interest rate risk, and inflation risk. It's important to carefully evaluate the credit quality of the bonds held in the fund, as well as the overall performance of the fund.

Municipal bond funds can be further categorized based on the maturity of the bonds held in the fund. Short-term municipal bond funds invest in bonds with maturities of one to three years, while intermediate-term municipal bond funds invest in bonds with maturities of three to ten years. Long-term municipal bond funds invest in bonds with maturities of more than ten years.

You should carefully consider your investment objectives and risk tolerance before investing in municipal bond funds. It's important to understand the potential risks and rewards of these funds and to seek the advice of a financial professional if needed.

4. HIGH-YIELD BOND FUNDS

High-yield bond funds, also known as junk bond funds, are mutual funds that invest in fixed-income securities that are rated below investment grade by major credit rating agencies.

These bonds have a higher default risk and, as a result, offer higher yields than investment-grade bonds.

High-yield bond funds invest in bonds issued by companies with a lower credit rating or non-investment grade companies. These companies are typically more leveraged and have a higher risk of default. High-yield bond funds may also invest in convertible bonds, which offer the potential for capital appreciation if the underlying stock price increases.

While high-yield bond funds offer the potential for higher returns, they also carry a higher level of risk. In times of economic uncertainty, the default rate on these bonds may increase, resulting in a decline in the value of the fund.

As a result, investors should carefully consider their risk tolerance before investing in high-yield bond funds. It is important to note that high-yield bond funds may not be suitable for all investors, and they should be used as part of a well-diversified investment portfolio.

ADVANTAGES OF DEBT FUNDS

1. **Lower Risk:** Debt funds are considered to be lower risk than equity funds due to their investment in fixed-income securities. This makes them a good option for investors who are looking for a more conservative investment option.

2. **Steady Income:** Debt funds provide a steady stream of income through interest payments, making them a good option for investors who are looking for a regular source of income.

3. **Diversification:** Debt funds provide diversification by investing in a portfolio of fixed-income securities across different sectors and industries.

4. **Liquidity:** Debt funds are highly liquid and can be bought and sold easily, making them a good choice for investors who need

access to their money quickly.

DISADVANTAGES OF DEBT FUNDS

1. **Lower Returns:** Debt funds typically provide lower returns than equity funds due to their lower risk.

2. **Inflation Risk:** Debt funds may be vulnerable to inflation risk, which can reduce the purchasing power of returns over time.

3. **Interest Rate Risk:** Debt funds may be impacted by changes in interest rates, which can impact the value of the fixed-income securities held by the fund.

4. **Credit Risk:** Debt funds may be impacted by changes in the creditworthiness of the issuers of the fixed-income securities held by the fund.

TIPS FOR INVESTING IN DEBT FUNDS

1. Consider your investment goals and risk tolerance before selecting a debt fund.

2. Do your research on the fund's performance history, management team, and fees before investing.

3. Diversify your portfolio by investing in a mix of government bond, corporate bond, municipal bond, and high-yield bond funds.

4. Regularly review your portfolio to ensure it aligns with your investment goals and make any necessary adjustments over time.

5. Be patient and focus on the long-term potential of debt funds, rather than short-term market fluctuations.

EXAMPLES AND CASE STUDIES

1. HDFC Short Term Debt Fund

This is a debt fund managed by HDFC Mutual Fund that invests in a diversified portfolio of debt and money market securities. The fund aims to provide investors with regular income while preserving capital. As of March 2023, the fund has delivered a one-year return of around 7.5%.

2. Franklin India Low Duration Fund

This is a low duration debt fund managed by Franklin Templeton Mutual Fund. The fund invests in debt and money market securities with a maturity of up to 1 year, which helps to reduce interest rate risk. As of March 2023, the fund has delivered a one-year return of around 6.5%.

3. Case Study

Debt Funds During COVID-19 - The outbreak of the COVID-19 pandemic in 2020 had a significant impact on financial markets worldwide. Debt funds, in particular, saw increased investor interest as the stock markets experienced volatility.

For instance, the HDFC Corporate Bond Fund, a debt fund managed by HDFC Mutual Fund, saw a surge in inflows during the pandemic due to its focus on high-quality corporate debt securities. The fund delivered a one-year return of around 9.5% as of March 2021.

4. Case Study

Interest Rate Risk in Debt Funds - Debt funds are subject to interest rate risk, which means that changes in interest rates can affect the value of the fund's investments. For instance, in 2013, the Reserve Bank of India (RBI) raised interest rates to combat inflation, which led to a decline in the NAVs of many debt funds.

The HDFC Short Term Opportunities Fund, a debt fund managed by HDFC Mutual Fund, saw its NAV decline by around 3% in a single day in July 2013 due to the RBI's policy actions.

5. Case Study

Credit Risk in Debt Funds - Debt funds are also subject to credit risk, which means that default by the issuer of the debt security can lead to a decline in the NAV of the fund.

For instance, in 2019, the IL&FS crisis in India led to a default on debt securities issued by the company, which had an impact on debt funds that held these securities. The UTI Credit Risk Fund, a debt fund managed by UTI Mutual Fund, saw a decline in its NAV due to exposure to IL&FS debt securities. The fund's NAV declined by around 4% in a single day in September 2018.

Debt funds can be a valuable investment option for investors seeking a steady stream of income and are willing to accept lower returns for lower risk. It is important to carefully consider the advantages and disadvantages of debt funds and to do your research before investing to ensure you select the best option for your investment goals and risk tolerance.

By diversifying your portfolio and regularly reviewing your investments, you can potentially maximize the benefits of debt funds over time.

5: HYBRID FUNDS

Hybrid funds, also known as balanced funds, are mutual funds that invest in both stocks and bonds. The goal of a hybrid fund is to provide you with a diversified portfolio that can potentially generate both income and capital appreciation.

Hybrid funds typically invest in a combination of stocks, bonds, and cash equivalents. The allocation of these assets can vary based on the fund's investment objective, risk profile, and market conditions.

For example, a conservative hybrid fund may have a higher allocation of bonds and cash equivalents, while an aggressive hybrid fund may have a higher allocation of stocks.

TYPES OF HYBRID FUNDS

1. CONSERVATIVE HYBRID FUNDS

Conservative hybrid funds are a type of hybrid fund that invests a higher proportion of their assets in debt securities or fixed income instruments, and a smaller portion in equities. The primary objective of these funds is to generate regular income for investors while preserving the capital invested.

Conservative hybrid funds are suitable for investors who are risk-averse and have a low-risk tolerance. These funds aim to provide a stable income stream while preserving the invested capital, making them an ideal investment option for retirees or investors who seek a steady income flow.

The asset allocation of conservative hybrid funds typically ranges from 75-80% in debt securities or fixed income instruments, such as government bonds, corporate bonds, and money market instruments, and the remaining 20-25% in equities. The allocation towards equities may vary depending on the market conditions and the fund manager's outlook.

Conservative hybrid funds are a suitable investment option for investors who seek regular income and capital preservation. However, investors should carefully consider the fund's asset allocation, risk profile, and expense ratio before investing in these funds. It is always recommended to consult a financial advisor before making any investment decisions.

2. BALANCED HYBRID FUNDS

Balanced hybrid funds, also known as balanced funds, are a type of hybrid fund that invests in both equities and debt securities in a balanced manner. The objective of balanced hybrid funds is to provide investors with both capital appreciation and regular income while maintaining a balance between the risk and returns of the portfolio.

The asset allocation of balanced hybrid funds typically ranges from 60-75% in equities and 25-40% in debt securities. The equity portion of the portfolio may include investments in large-cap, mid-cap, or small-cap companies across various sectors. The debt securities portion of the portfolio may include investments in government bonds, corporate bonds, and money market instruments.

Balanced hybrid funds are a suitable investment option for investors who seek a balanced investment portfolio with a moderate level of risk. These funds may be appropriate for investors who are looking to diversify their investments and want exposure to both equities and fixed income securities.

However, investors should carefully consider the asset allocation, risk profile, and investment objective of the fund before investing. It is always recommended to consult a financial advisor before making any investment decisions.

3. AGGRESSIVE HYBRID FUNDS

Aggressive hybrid funds, also known as equity-oriented hybrid funds, are a type of hybrid fund that invests a larger proportion of its assets in equities and a smaller portion in debt securities. These funds aim to provide investors with the potential for higher returns through equity investments while also providing some level of capital preservation through the fixed income investments.

The asset allocation of aggressive hybrid funds typically ranges from 65-80% in equities and 20-35% in debt securities. The equity portion of the portfolio may include investments in large-cap, mid-cap, or small-cap companies across various sectors. The debt securities portion of the portfolio may include investments in government bonds, corporate bonds, and money market instruments.

Aggressive hybrid funds are a suitable investment option for investors who are willing to take on a higher level of risk in pursuit of higher returns. These funds may be appropriate for investors who have a moderate to high-risk tolerance and a longer investment horizon. However, higher allocation towards equities in aggressive hybrid funds also exposes investors to higher market risk and volatility.

The performance of aggressive hybrid funds is influenced by the fund manager 's investment decisions and the overall market conditions. It is important to research and evaluate the fund manager's track record, investment strategy, and the fund's past performance before investing.

Additionally, you need to consider your investment goals,

financial situation, and risk tolerance before investing in aggressive hybrid funds. Consult with a financial advisor to determine whether aggressive hybrid funds are suitable for their investment needs.

ADVANTAGES OF HYBRID FUNDS:

1. **Diversification**: Hybrid funds provide investors with a diversified portfolio of assets, which can help reduce overall risk.

2. **Professional Management**: Hybrid funds are managed by experienced professionals who monitor market conditions and adjust the fund's asset allocation to maximize returns and minimize risk.

3. **Flexibility**: Hybrid funds offer investors the flexibility to choose a fund that aligns with their investment goals and risk tolerance.

4. **Potential for Higher Returns**: Hybrid funds have the potential to generate higher returns than fixed-income securities alone, while still providing a level of safety.

DISADVANTAGES OF HYBRID FUNDS

1. **Fees**: Like all mutual funds, hybrid funds charge management fees, which can eat into investment returns.

2. **Market Volatility**: Although hybrid funds provide some protection against market volatility, they can still be impacted by shifts in market conditions.

3. **Risk of Loss**: Hybrid funds, like all investment products, carry the risk of loss. The level of risk varies based on the fund's asset allocation and market conditions.

EXAMPLES AND CASE STUDIES

1. HDFC HYBRID EQUITY FUND

The HDFC Hybrid Equity Fund is a popular hybrid fund that invests in a mix of equity and debt instruments. The fund aims to provide long-term capital appreciation by investing primarily in equity and equity-related instruments while also providing income from fixed-income securities. As of March 2023, the fund has delivered a return of over 19% in the past year and has consistently outperformed its benchmark over the past few years.

2. SBI EQUITY HYBRID FUND

The SBI Equity Hybrid Fund is another well-known hybrid fund that invests in a mix of equity and debt instruments. The fund aims to generate long-term capital appreciation while also providing income from fixed-income securities. As of March 2023, the fund has delivered a return of over 18% in the past year and has consistently outperformed its benchmark over the past few years.

CASE STUDIES

Rowe Price Capital Appreciation Fund

The T Rowe Price Capital Appreciation Fund is a hybrid fund that invests in a mix of equities, fixed-income securities, and cash. The fund aims to provide long-term capital growth and income by investing in a diversified portfolio of stocks and bonds. In 2020, when the COVID-19 pandemic hit and the markets crashed, the fund was able to weather the storm and deliver a positive return for the year. This was largely due to the fund's diversified portfolio, which helped to cushion the impact of the market downturn.

Franklin India Hybrid Equity Fund

The Franklin India Hybrid Equity Fund is a hybrid fund that invests primarily in equity and equity-related securities, with a small allocation to fixed-income instruments. In 2018, when the IL&FS crisis hit and the markets tumbled, the fund suffered a significant decline in its net asset value (NAV).

However, the fund's managers quickly responded by reducing the fund's exposure to risky debt instruments and increasing its allocation to cash and high-quality fixed-income securities. As a result, the fund was able to recover its losses and deliver a positive return for the year. This case study highlights the importance of active management and risk management in hybrid funds.

***

Hybrid funds can be a good option for investors seeking a diversified portfolio that provides both income and capital appreciation potential.

However, you should carefully consider the fund's investment objective, risk profile, and fees before investing. It's important to consult with a financial advisor to determine if a hybrid fund aligns with your investment goals and risk tolerance.

6: INDEX FUNDS

I ndex funds are mutual funds that track a specific market index, such such as the S&P 500, the Dow Jones Industrial Average, or the NASDAQ. These funds aim to replicate the performance of the index they track, rather than trying to outperform it. As a result, they offer investors a low-cost and passive way to invest in the stock market.

Index funds typically have lower management fees than actively managed funds since they don't require the same level of research and analysis by fund managers.

They also tend to have lower turnover rates since they only need to make adjustments to their portfolio when the underlying index changes.

TYPES OF INDEX FUNDS:

1. STOCK INDEX FUNDS

Stock index funds are designed to replicate the performance of its target index by investing in the same stocks that are included in the index. The fund's portfolio manager aims to match the index's performance by buying and holding the same stocks in the same proportion as the index.

Stock index funds are a popular investment option for investors who are looking for a low-cost, passive investment strategy that aims to provide broad market exposure. Unlike actively managed funds, which employ portfolio managers to select individual stocks, stock index funds don't rely on stock picking or market timing. Instead, they aim to replicate the performance of the overall market or a specific segment of the market.

Stock index funds are often used as a benchmark for active fund managers to measure their performance against. They can also be used as a core holding in a diversified investment portfolio, as they provide exposure to a broad range of stocks with lower expenses and typically outperform actively managed funds over the long term.

Overall, stock index funds can provide a simple, low-cost way to invest in the stock market and capture its long-term growth potential.

2. BOND INDEX FUNDS

Bond index funds track the performance of a bond index, such as the Barclays U.S. Aggregate Bond Index or the Bloomberg Barclays Global Aggregate Bond Index. These funds invest in a diversified portfolio of bonds that match the index's composition, with the goal of delivering returns similar to those of the index.

Bond index funds can be further classified based on the type of bonds they invest in. For example, a U.S. Treasury bond index fund invests solely in U.S. Treasury bonds, while a corporate bond index fund invests in bonds issued by corporations.

One advantage of bond index funds is that they provide investors with exposure to a diversified portfolio of bonds, which can help reduce overall risk. They also tend to have lower fees compared to actively managed bond funds, as they do not require a portfolio manager to make buying and selling decisions.

However, it's important to note that bond index funds are still subject to interest rate risk, credit risk, and other risks associated with investing in bonds. It's also possible for a bond index fund to underperform its benchmark index due to factors such as tracking error or fees.

As with any investment, it's important to do your research and consider your individual investment goals and risk tolerance before investing in a bond index fund.

3. INTERNATIONAL INDEX FUNDS

International index funds are designed to track the performance of an international stock market index, which is usually based on a specific geographic region or a combination of regions. For example, the MSCI EAFE Index tracks the performance of large and mid-cap stocks in developed markets outside of North America, including Europe, Asia, and Australia.

By investing in an international index fund, investors can gain exposure to a diversified portfolio of stocks from multiple countries and industries. The fund's portfolio is typically weighted based on the market capitalization of the underlying stocks, meaning that larger companies have a greater impact on the fund's performance than smaller companies.

One advantage of investing in international index funds is that they provide investors with a cost-effective way to gain exposure to a diverse set of international stocks. Investing in international index funds can help to mitigate the risk associated with investing in individual stocks or companies, as the fund's portfolio is diversified across multiple countries and industries.

Another advantage of investing in international index funds is that they offer investors the opportunity to participate in the growth potential of international markets. As developing economies continue to expand, there may be opportunities for companies in those regions to experience significant growth, which can translate into higher returns for investors who have exposure to those markets through international index funds.

However, it's important to note that investing in international index funds also carries risks. Changes in exchange rates, geopolitical events, and regulatory changes in different countries can all impact the performance of the fund. Additionally, different regions and industries may have varying levels of risk and volatility.

Carefully consider your investment objectives and risk tolerance before investing in international index funds. It's also important to research the specific index that the fund tracks and understand its composition, including the geographic regions and industries represented.

ADVANTAGES OF INDEX FUNDS

1. **Low Cost**: Index funds typically have lower management fees than actively managed funds, which can help investors keep more of their investment returns.

2. **Diversification**: Index funds provide investors with exposure to a diversified portfolio of stocks or bonds, which can help reduce overall risk.

3. **Passive Management**: Index funds are passively managed, which means they don't require the same level of research and analysis as actively managed funds.

4. **Consistent Returns**: Index funds aim to replicate the performance of the index they track, which can lead to more consistent returns over the long term.

DISADVANTAGES OF INDEX FUNDS

1. **Limited Upside Potential**: Since index funds aim to replicate the performance of the index they track, investors won't be able to benefit from the potential outperformance of individual stocks.

2. **Lack of Flexibility**: Index funds are limited to the stocks or bonds in the index they track, which means they may not be able to take advantage of emerging trends or industries.

3. **Market Risk**: Index funds are still subject to market risk, which means they can lose value if the overall market experiences a downturn.

EXAMPLES AND CASE STUDIES

Vanguard 500 Index Fund

The Vanguard 500 Index Fund is one of the most well-known index funds in the world. It tracks the S&P 500 index, which is a market-cap-weighted index of 500 of the largest publicly traded companies in the United States. The fund has a low expense ratio of 0.14%, which makes it a popular choice for investors looking to invest in large-cap US equities at a low cost.

iShares MSCI EAFE ETF

The iShares MSCI EAFE ETF is an index fund that tracks the MSCI EAFE index, which is a market-cap-weighted index of companies in developed markets outside of North America, including Europe, Australia, and Asia. The fund has a low expense ratio of 0.32%, making it a popular choice for investors looking to invest in international equities at a low cost.

Fidelity US Bond Index Fund

The Fidelity US Bond Index Fund is an index fund that tracks the Bloomberg Barclays US Aggregate Bond index, which is a broad-based index of US investment-grade bonds. The fund has a low expense ratio of 0.025%, making it a popular choice for investors looking to invest in US fixed income at a low cost.

Index funds can be a good option if you want to achieve long-term returns through a low-cost, passive investment strategy. They offer diversification, consistency, and low management fees, which can help you to keep more of your investment returns.

However, index funds do have limitations, including limited upside potential and lack of flexibility, and they are still subject to market risk. Ultimately, you should consider your investment goals and risk tolerance when deciding whether or not to invest in index funds.

7: SECTOR FUNDS

Sector funds are mutual funds that focus on specific sectors or industries, such as technology, healthcare, or energy. These funds invest in companies that operate within the chosen sector or industry, giving investors exposure to that particular segment of the economy.

TYPES OF SECTOR FUNDS:

1. TECHNOLOGY SECTOR FUNDS

Technology sector funds are mutual funds that focus primarily on investing in technology companies. These companies are typically involved in the development and production of hardware, software, telecommunications, and other technology-related products and services.

Investing in technology sector funds can provide investors with a way to potentially benefit from the rapid pace of technological innovation and growth in the technology sector. As technology continues to transform industries and societies, companies in this sector may be poised for continued growth and success, leading to potential investment returns for investors.

However, it's important to note that investing in technology sector funds also carries risks. The technology sector can be highly volatile, with rapid changes in market trends and disruptions to established business models. Additionally, some technology companies may be highly concentrated in specific sub-sectors or reliant on a few key products or services, which can increase the fund's risk.

You need to carefully consider your investment objectives and risk tolerance before investing in technology sector funds. It's also important to research the specific fund and its holdings to ensure that it aligns with your goals and objectives.

2. HEALTHCARE SECTOR FUNDS

Healthcare sector funds are mutual funds that focus primarily on investing in companies that are involved in the healthcare industry, including companies that produce pharmaceuticals, medical devices, and healthcare services.

Investing in healthcare sector funds can provide investors with a way to potentially benefit from the growth and innovation in the healthcare industry. As the global population ages and demand for healthcare services continues to increase, healthcare companies may be poised for continued growth and success, leading to potential investment returns for investors.

However, investing in healthcare sector funds also carries risks. The healthcare industry can be highly regulated, and changes in government policies and regulations can impact the industry's performance. Additionally, healthcare companies may be subject to clinical trial failures, patent expirations, and other risks that can impact their financial performance and the fund's returns.

Carefully consider your investment objectives and risk tolerance before investing in healthcare sector funds. It's also important to evaluate the fund's fees, past performance, and investment strategy to ensure that it aligns with your investment goals and values.

Furthermore, it's essential to diversify your portfolio and not rely solely on one sector, such as healthcare. By spreading your investments across different sectors, you can reduce your overall risk and potentially increase your returns.

3. ENERGY SECTOR FUNDS

Healthcare sector funds are mutual funds that focus primarily on investing in companies that are involved in the healthcare industry, including companies that produce pharmaceuticals, medical devices, and healthcare services.

Investing in healthcare sector funds can provide investors with a way to potentially benefit from the growth and innovation in the healthcare industry. As the global population ages and demand for healthcare services continues to increase, healthcare companies may be poised for continued growth and success, leading to potential investment returns.

However, investing in healthcare sector funds also carries risks. The healthcare industry can be highly regulated, and changes in government policies and regulations can impact the industry's performance. Additionally, healthcare companies may be subject to clinical trial failures, patent expirations, and other risks that can impact their financial performance and the fund's returns.

Consider your investment objectives and risk tolerance before investing in healthcare sector funds. It's also important to evaluate the fund's fees, past performance, and investment strategy to ensure that it aligns with your investment goals and values.

Furthermore, it's essential to diversify your portfolio and not rely solely on one sector, such as healthcare. By spreading your investments across different sectors, you can reduce your overall risk and potentially increase your returns.

4. CONSUMER DISCRETIONARY SECTOR FUNDS

Consumer discretionary sector funds are a type of mutual fund that invests primarily in companies that produce goods and services that are considered non-essential or discretionary purchases, such as clothing, luxury goods, automobiles, entertainment, and travel companies.

Companies in this sector may be more sensitive to changes in consumer spending patterns, which can be influenced by economic conditions, consumer confidence, and trends in popular culture.

Consumer discretionary sector funds may be attractive to investors who believe that consumer spending will continue to grow over time, as the economy expands and incomes rise.

Additionally, companies in this sector may benefit from changes in consumer preferences and shifting demographics, as younger generations become more important consumers of new and innovative products and services.

However, investing in consumer discretionary sector funds also carries risks. Consumer spending patterns can be impacted by a wide range of factors, including changes in economic conditions, shifts in consumer preferences, and disruptions to traditional business models due to technological innovation.

Additionally, companies in this sector may be subject to strong competition and rapid changes in popular culture and trends, which can make it challenging to maintain market share and profitability over time. Therefore, you should carefully consider your risk tolerance and investment goals before investing in consumer discretionary sector funds.

It is also important to note that consumer discretionary sector funds are typically more volatile than other types of mutual funds, such as those that invest in companies in the consumer staples or utilities sectors. This is because companies in the discretionary sector are often more closely tied to overall economic conditions, and may experience more significant swings in performance during times of economic uncertainty or market volatility.

Consumer discretionary sector funds can be an attractive option if you are looking to gain exposure to companies that produce non-essential goods and services. However, carefully consider the risks and potential rewards associated with investing in this sector, and ensure that your investment strategy aligns with your goals and risk tolerance.

5. FINANCIAL SECTOR FUNDS

Financial sector funds are a type of mutual fund that primarily invest in companies within the financial sector, such as banks, insurance companies, investment firms, and other financial institutions. These funds are designed to provide investors with exposure to companies within the financial industry and may be attractive to investors who believe that the financial sector will perform well over time.

The financial sector is a crucial part of the economy and plays a significant role in the allocation of capital and the management of risk. Companies within the financial sector may benefit from economic growth and stability, as well as from changes in interest rates, monetary policy, and regulatory developments.

However, investing in financial sector funds also carries certain risks. Financial companies may be exposed to regulatory, legal, and reputational risks, which can impact their performance and profitability. Additionally, companies within the financial sector may be susceptible to changes in interest rates, credit markets, and global economic conditions, which can impact their business models and financial stability.

If you are considering investing in financial sector funds, carefully evaluate your investment objectives, risk tolerance, and time horizon before making a decision. It is also important to carefully evaluate the management team and track record of the mutual fund, as well as the fees and expenses associated with investing in the fund.

6. REAL ESTATE SECTOR FUNDS

Real estate sector funds are a type of mutual fund that primarily invest in companies involved in the real estate industry, such as real estate investment trusts (REITs), home builders, and companies involved in property management and development. These funds are designed to provide investors with exposure to the real estate industry, which can offer diversification benefits and potential for capital appreciation and income.

Real estate is an essential part of the economy and plays a critical role in providing housing, commercial space, and other essential infrastructure. Companies within the real estate sector may benefit from population growth, economic expansion, and trends in urbanization and demographic shifts.

However, investing in real estate sector funds also carries certain risks. Companies within the real estate industry may be impacted by changes in interest rates, fluctuations in property values, and regulatory developments.

Additionally, real estate sector funds may be subject to liquidity risks, as real estate investments can be difficult to buy or sell quickly in times of market volatility.

If you are considering investing in real estate sector funds, carefully evaluate your investment objectives, risk tolerance, and time horizon before making a decision. It is also important to carefully evaluate the management team and track record of the mutual fund, as well as the fees and expenses associated with investing in the fund.

ADVANTAGES OF SECTOR FUNDS

1. **Diversification within a Specific Sector**: Sector funds provide investors with exposure to a specific sector or industry, which can help diversify their portfolio.

2. **Potential for Higher Returns**: Sector funds have the potential for higher returns than broader market funds if the chosen sector performs well.

3. **Targeted Investing**: Sector funds allow investors to target specific industries or sectors they believe have strong growth potential.

4. **Professional Management**: Sector funds are managed by professional fund managers who have experience in investing

within a specific sector or industry.

DISADVANTAGES OF SECTOR FUNDS

1. **High Risk**: Sector funds are riskier than broader market funds since they focus on a specific sector or industry.

2. **Limited Diversification**: Sector funds are less diversified than broader market funds since they only invest in companies within a specific sector or industry.

3. **Volatility**: Sector funds can be more volatile than broader market funds since they are tied to the performance of a specific sector or industry.

4. **Higher Expenses**: Sector funds may have higher expenses than broader market funds since they require more research and analysis by fund managers.

EXAMPLES AND CASE STUDIES

1. Technology Sector Fund

The Vanguard Information Technology ETF (VGT) is an example of a technology sector fund. This fund invests in companies within the technology sector such as Apple, Microsoft, and Alphabet (Google). As of March 2023, VGT has a 5-year average annual return of 33.18%.

2. Healthcare Sector Fund

The Fidelity MSCI Health Care Index ETF (FHLC) is an example of a healthcare sector fund. This fund invests in companies within the healthcare sector such as Johnson & Johnson, Pfizer, and UnitedHealth Group. As of March 2023, FHLC has a 5-year average annual return of 15.74%.

3. Energy Sector Fund

The Energy Select Sector SPDR Fund (XLE) is an example of an energy sector fund. This fund invests in companies within the energy sector such as Exxon Mobil, Chevron, and ConocoPhillips. As of March 2023, XLE has a 5-year average annual return of 3.38%.

4. Real Estate Sector Fund

The Vanguard Real Estate ETF (VNQ) is an example of a real estate sector fund. This fund invests in companies within the real estate sector such as American Tower, Prologis, and Simon Property Group. As of March 2023, VNQ has a 5-year average annual return of 7.56%.

Sector funds can be a good option if you want to target specific sectors or industries within the market. However, be aware of the higher risk and limited diversification associated with these funds. It's important to carefully consider your investment goals and risk tolerance before investing in sector funds.

Additionally, it's a good idea to combine sector funds with other types of mutual funds in order to create a well-diversified portfolio. As with any investment, it's important to do your research and seek advice from a financial professional before making any investment decisions.

8: INTERNATIONAL FUNDS

International funds are mutual funds that invest in companies outside of your home country. These funds provide investors with exposure to foreign markets and can help diversify their portfolio beyond domestic investments.

International funds can invest in developed or emerging markets, and the degree of risk and potential return can vary based on the regions and countries they invest in.

TYPES OF INTERNATIONAL FUNDS

1. INTERNATIONAL EQUITY FUNDS

International equity funds are a specific type of international fund that invests primarily in stocks of foreign companies. These funds may also be referred to as global equity funds or foreign equity funds.

International equity funds provide investors with exposure to companies outside of their home country, which can offer diversification benefits and potentially higher returns. By investing in international stocks, investors can take advantage of the growth potential of companies in emerging markets, as well as the stability of established companies in developed markets.

International equity funds may focus on a specific region, such as Europe, Asia, or Latin America, or they may invest globally across multiple regions. Some funds may also focus on a particular sector, such as technology or healthcare.

Investing in international equity funds involves additional risks compared to investing solely in domestic equity funds. These risks may include currency fluctuations, political instability, and differences in accounting standards and regulations.

As with any investment, it is important to carefully consider your investment goals, risk tolerance, and investment time horizon before investing in international equity funds.

2. GLOBAL EQUITY FUNDS

Global equity funds are a type of international fund that invests in stocks of companies located around the world, including both domestic and foreign companies. Unlike international equity funds, which focus solely on foreign stocks, global equity funds invest in a mix of both domestic and foreign stocks.

Global equity funds aim to provide investors with exposure to a wide range of global investment opportunities, with the goal of achieving long-term capital appreciation. These funds may invest in both developed and emerging markets, as well as a variety of sectors and industries.

One benefit of investing in global equity funds is that they offer a high degree of diversification, since they invest in companies located around the world. This can help to reduce risk and volatility in an investor's portfolio, as economic and political conditions in one country or region may have less of an impact on the overall portfolio performance.

Global equity funds, like all investments, involve some degree of risk. Currency fluctuations, political instability, and changes in global economic conditions can all impact the performance of these funds.

It is important to carefully consider your investment goals, risk tolerance, and investment time horizon before investing in global equity funds, and to consult with a financial advisor if needed.

3. REGIONAL FUNDS

Regional funds are a type of international fund that invests primarily in stocks or other securities of companies located in a specific geographic region.

These funds can focus on a particular country or region, such as Europe, Asia, or Latin America. They may also invest in a particular sector or industry within that region.

One benefit of investing in regional funds is that they provide investors with exposure to a specific area of the world, which can allow investors to take advantage of growth potential or stability in that region. Regional funds can also provide diversification benefits by investing in a variety of companies within a particular region.

However, regional funds can also be subject to additional risks. For example, political instability or economic downturns in a specific region can have a negative impact on the performance of the fund. Currency fluctuations may also affect the value of the fund's holdings, especially if the fund invests in companies denominated in foreign currencies.

It is important you carefully consider your investment goals, risk tolerance, and investment time horizon before investing in regional funds. Also research the economic and political conditions in the region in which the fund invests, as well as the companies held in the fund's portfolio, to better understand the potential risks and rewards associated with the investment.

You may also want to consult with a financial advisor to determine if regional funds are appropriate for their investment objectives.

4. EMERGING MARKETS FUNDS

Emerging markets funds are a type of international fund that invests primarily in stocks or other securities of companies located in developing countries or emerging economies. These funds may focus on a particular region or country, such as Brazil, China, or India, or they may invest across multiple emerging markets.

Investing in emerging markets funds can offer investors the potential for higher returns, as emerging markets may experience faster economic growth and offer greater opportunities for capital appreciation.

However, investing in emerging markets can also involve higher risks, as these markets may be subject to political instability, currency fluctuations, and weaker regulatory environments.

Emerging markets funds may also invest in a variety of sectors and industries, such as technology, consumer goods, or financial services. Some emerging markets funds may also invest in small or mid-cap companies, which can offer greater potential for growth but also involve higher risks.

Carefully consider your investment goals, risk tolerance, and investment time horizon before investing in emerging markets funds. You should also be aware of the potential risks associated with investing in emerging markets, including currency risk, political risk, and liquidity risk. It may be appropriate to consult with a financial advisor to determine if investing in emerging markets funds is appropriate for you.

ADVANTAGES OF INTERNATIONAL FUNDS

1. **Diversification**: International funds provide investors with exposure to foreign markets, which can help diversify their portfolio and reduce risk.

2. **Growth Potential**: International funds provide access to companies with high growth potential that may not be available in the investor's home country.

3. **Currency Diversification**: International funds can provide investors with currency diversification, which can help mitigate the impact of currency fluctuations on their investments.

4. **Professional Management**: International funds are managed by professional fund managers who have expertise in investing in foreign markets.

DISADVANTAGES OF INTERNATIONAL FUNDS

1. **Market Risk**: International funds are subject to market risk, which means they can lose value if the overall market experiences a downturn.

2. **Exchange Rate Risk**: International funds are also subject to exchange rate risk, which means the value of the investor's investment may be impacted by changes in foreign currency exchange rates.

3. **Political Risk**: International funds may be exposed to political risk, such as changes in government policies or regulations, which can impact the value of the investments.

4. **Higher Expenses**: International funds may have higher expenses than domestic funds due to additional research and analysis required by fund managers.

EXAMPLES AND CASE STUDIES

1. Vanguard Total International Stock Index Fund (VGTSX)

This fund invests in stocks of companies located in developed and emerging markets outside of the United States. It tracks the performance of the FTSE Global All Cap ex US Index, providing investors with exposure to a diversified mix of international equities.

2. Fidelity Emerging Markets Fund (FEMKX)

This fund invests in stocks of companies located in emerging markets such as China, India, Brazil, and South Africa. It aims to provide investors with long-term capital appreciation through exposure to high-growth potential markets.

3. T. Rowe Price International Discovery Fund (PRIDX)

This fund invests in stocks of small and mid-cap companies located in developed and emerging markets outside of the United States. It aims to provide investors with long-term capital growth through exposure to companies with high growth potential.

CASE STUDIES:

1. Emerging Markets Growth

In the early 2000s, emerging markets such as China and India were experiencing rapid economic growth. This growth led to increased demand for goods and services, resulting in significant investment opportunities. Investors who invested in international funds with exposure to emerging markets during this time period, such as the Fidelity Emerging Markets Fund, were able to capture the high returns that these markets offered.

2. European Debt Crisis

In the late 2000s, Europe experienced a debt crisis that resulted in significant economic instability. Investors who held international funds with exposure to European markets, such as the Vanguard Total International Stock Index Fund, may have experienced a decline in their investment returns during this time period. However, investors who held a diversified portfolio of international funds were better able to weather the storm and may have still experienced overall positive returns.

3. Japanese Recovery

In the 2010s, Japan implemented policies to stimulate economic growth, resulting in a period of strong economic performance. Investors who held international funds with exposure to Japanese markets, such as the T. Rowe Price International Discovery Fund, may have benefited from the recovery of the Japanese economy and experienced strong returns during this time period.

International funds can be a good option for you if you

want to diversify your portfolio and gain exposure to foreign markets. However, you should be aware of the risks associated with investing in foreign markets and carefully consider your investment objectives and risk tolerance before investing in international funds.

9: MONEY MARKET FUNDS

Money market funds are a type of mutual fund that invests in short-term, low-risk securities such as Treasury bills, certificates of deposit, and commercial paper.

These funds aim to provide you with a safe and stable return on your investment, while maintaining a high level of liquidity.

TYPES OF MONEY MARKET FUNDS

1. GOVERNMENT MONEY MARKET FUNDS

Government money market funds are a specific type of money market fund that invests primarily in short-term debt issued by the US government or its agencies. These funds typically invest in Treasury bills and bonds, which are considered the safest and most liquid of all government securities.

Investing in government money market funds can provide investors with a number of benefits.

First, these funds are generally considered to be very low-risk investments, as they invest in securities that are backed by the US government. This means that investors are unlikely to lose money on their investment and can have a high degree of confidence in the stability of their investment.

Second, government money market funds are highly liquid, which means that investors can easily buy and sell shares of the fund as needed. This can be particularly useful for investors who need access to their funds quickly and do not want to be tied up in long-term investments.

Third, government money market funds can provide investors with a higher yield than other types of short-term investments, such as savings accounts or CDs. While the yield on government money market funds is generally lower than other types of mutual funds, it is still higher than many other short-term investment options.

However, government money market funds are not completely risk-free. While the securities they invest in are backed by the US government, there is still a risk of default or other financial instability that could impact the fund's performance.

2. TAX-EXEMPT MONEY MARKET FUNDS

Tax-exempt money market funds are a type of mutual fund that invests in short-term, low-risk securities such as municipal bonds. These funds aim to provide investors with a stable investment option that is also tax-free at the federal and, in some cases, state level.

Municipal bonds are issued by state and local governments to finance public projects such as schools, highways, and hospitals. These bonds are generally exempt from federal income tax and, depending on the state of issue and the residence of the investor, may also be exempt from state and local taxes. This tax-exempt status allows you to earn a higher after-tax yield than you would with taxable investments.

Investing in tax-exempt money market funds can provide you with a number of benefits.

First, these funds are generally considered to be very low-risk investments, as they invest in securities that are backed by state and local governments. This means that you are unlikely to lose money on your investment and can have a high degree of confidence in the stability of your investment.

Second, tax-exempt money market funds can provide you with a higher after-tax yield than other types of short-term investments, such as savings accounts or CDs. This can be particularly beneficial if you are in the higher tax brackets, looking for ways to reduce your tax liability.

Third, tax-exempt money market funds are highly liquid, which means that you can easily buy and sell shares of the fund as needed. This can be particularly useful if you need access to your funds quickly and do not want to be tied up in long-term investments.

However, tax-exempt money market funds are not completely risk-free. While the securities they invest in are backed by state and local governments, there is still a risk of default or other financial instability that could impact the fund's performance.

3. PRIME MONEY MARKET FUNDS

Prime money market funds are a type of mutual fund that invests in short-term, low-risk securities such as commercial paper, certificates of deposit, and Treasury bills. These funds are designed to provide you with a slightly higher yield than other types of money market funds, such as government and tax-exempt money market funds, while still maintaining a high level of safety.

Commercial paper is a type of short-term debt issued by corporations to finance their day-to-day operations, while certificates of deposit are issued by banks to raise funds. Treasury bills are short-term debt securities issued by the U.S. government.

Prime money market funds may offer slightly higher yields than other money market funds because they invest in securities that are not necessarily backed by the full faith and credit of the U.S. government. However, they are still considered to be relatively low-risk investments, as the securities they invest in are generally highly rated and have a low risk of default.

Prime money market funds can provide you with a number of benefits.

First, they offer a higher yield than other types of money market funds, which can be attractive to investors looking for a slightly higher return on their investment.

Second, prime money market funds are highly liquid, which means that you can easily buy and sell shares of the fund as needed. This can be particularly useful if you need access to your funds quickly and do not want to be tied up in long-term investments.

Third, prime money market funds are generally considered to be very safe investments, as they invest in securities that are highly rated and have a low risk of default. This makes them a good option if you are looking for a low-risk investment option.

However, prime money market funds are not completely risk-free. While they are generally considered to be low-risk investments, there is still a risk of default or other financial instability that could impact the fund's performance.

ADVANTAGES OF MONEY MARKET FUNDS

1. **Stability**: Money market funds are considered low-risk investments, making them a popular option for investors who want a stable return on their investment.

2. **Liquidity**: Money market funds are highly liquid, which means investors can easily access their money when they need it.

3. **Diversification**: Money market funds provide investors with a diversified portfolio of short-term debt securities, which can help reduce overall risk.

4. **Low Fees**: Money market funds typically have low management fees since they invest in low-risk, low-cost securities.

DISADVANTAGES OF MONEY MARKET FUNDS

1. **Low Returns**: Money market funds provide a lower return than other types of mutual funds, making them less attractive to investors who are looking for higher returns.

2. Inflation Risk: Money market funds are subject to inflation risk, which means that the returns may not keep up with inflation over the long term.

3. Interest Rate Risk: Money market funds are subject to interest rate risk, which means that the returns may be negatively affected by changes in interest rates.

4. Limited Upside Potential: Money market funds provide limited upside potential since they invest in low-risk securities.

EXAMPLES AND CASE STUDIES

1. Vanguard Prime Money Market Fund

This fund is an example of a Prime Money Market Fund that invests in short-term, high-quality securities issued by banks, corporations, and the US government. The fund has a current yield of around 0.05% and a low expense ratio of 0.16%. It's considered a safe and stable investment option for investors who want a low-risk, liquid investment.

2. Fidelity Government Money Market Fund

This fund is an example of a Government Money Market Fund that invests in short-term US government securities. The fund has a current yield of around 0.01% and a low expense ratio of 0.42%. It's a good option for investors who want to invest in low-risk, high-quality securities issued by the US government.

3. Schwab Municipal Money Fund

This fund is an example of a Tax-Exempt Money Market Fund that invests in short-term debt securities issued by state and local governments. The fund has a current yield of around 0.01% and a low expense ratio of 0.26%. It's a good option for investors who want to invest in tax-exempt securities issued by state and local governments.

***

Money market funds can be a good option if you are looking for a low-risk, stable return on your investment with high liquidity. However, they may not be the best option if you are looking for higher returns or are willing to take on more risk.

As with any investment, it's important to consider your individual investment goals and risk tolerance before investing in a money market fund.

10: MUTUAL FUND EXPENSES

FEES, CHARGES, AND EXPENSE RATIO

Mutual funds come with a variety of expenses, fees, and charges that can affect an investor's returns. In this chapter, we will explore the various types of expenses associated with mutual funds.

1. SALES CHARGES

Sales charges, also known as loads, are fees charged to investors when they purchase or sell shares of a mutual fund. These charges are paid to the broker or financial advisor who facilitates the transaction. There are two types of sales charges: front-end loads and back-end loads.

Front-end loads are charges that are assessed at the time of purchase, and they are typically a percentage of the amount invested.

For example, if an investor purchases $10,000 worth of a mutual fund with a front-end load of 5%, then $500 will be deducted from the investment and $9,500 will be invested in the fund.

Back-end loads, also known as contingent deferred sales charges (CDSC), are assessed when an investor sells their shares. The fee typically decreases over time, so the longer an investor holds the shares, the lower the fee will be.

For example, a mutual fund may have a CDSC of 5% if shares are sold within the first year, 4% if sold within the second year, and so on until the fee is eventually reduced to zero.

Sales charges can have a significant impact on an investor's returns, particularly in the long term. Investors should be aware of the fees associated with a mutual fund before investing and consider whether the potential returns justify the costs.

It's also important to note that not all mutual funds charge sales fees, and there are many no-load funds available for investors who want to avoid these charges.

2. MANAGEMENT FEES

Management fees are a type of operating expense that mutual funds charge investors to cover the cost of managing and operating the fund. The management fee is calculated as a percentage of the fund's assets under management (AUM) and is typically paid annually.

The management fee covers various expenses, including the salaries of the fund's management team and other personnel, as well as administrative costs such as legal fees and rent. Management fees also cover expenses related to research and analysis of potential investments, as well as ongoing monitoring of the fund's portfolio.

The amount of the management fee varies depending on the mutual fund and can range from less than 0.1% to over 2% of AUM. For example, a fund with $1 billion in assets under management and a management fee of 1% would charge investors $10 million in management fees per year.

While management fees may seem like a small percentage of the total investment, they can have a significant impact on an investor's returns over time. Higher fees mean less money is available to be invested and earn returns.

Therefore, you should carefully consider the management fees associated with a mutual fund before investing and compare them to other similar funds to ensure you are getting good value for your money.

3. EXPENSE RATIO

Expense ratio is a measure of the total cost of owning a mutual fund, expressed as a percentage of the fund's average net assets. The expense ratio includes all the operating expenses and shareholder fees that a mutual fund charges, including management fees, administrative expenses, and other costs such as audit fees and legal fees.

The expense ratio is a critical factor to consider when investing in a mutual fund as it directly impacts the investor's returns. For example, if a fund has an expense ratio of 1%, an investor with a $10,000 investment will pay $100 in fees annually, regardless of whether the fund generates any returns. Therefore, a lower expense ratio is generally better for investors.

Expense ratios can vary widely depending on the mutual fund and its investment strategy. Actively managed funds, which have a management team actively making investment decisions, typically have higher expense ratios than passively managed index funds, which seek to replicate the performance of a benchmark index.

The expense ratio for an actively managed fund can be as high as 2% or more, while index funds typically have expense ratios under 0.5%.

In addition to the management fees and other operating expenses, some mutual funds also charge shareholder fees such as sales loads and 12b-1 fees. These fees are included in the expense ratio calculation and can add significantly to the cost of owning the fund.

When evaluating mutual funds, investors should compare the expense ratios of different funds to identify those with lower costs. However, it's also essential to consider other factors such as the fund's investment strategy, past performance, and risk profile before making an investment decision.

4. OTHER FEES AND CHARGES

In addition to the sales charges, management fees, and expense ratios discussed earlier, mutual funds may also charge other fees and expenses. These fees and expenses can include:

1. **Redemption Fees**: These fees are charged when an investor sells shares of a mutual fund, usually within a specific time frame after purchase. The fee is intended to discourage short-term trading and can be a percentage of the sale price or a flat fee.

2. **Exchange Fees**: Some mutual funds allow investors to exchange shares of one fund for shares of another fund within the same fund family. Exchange fees are charged for this transaction and can vary depending on the fund.

3. **Account Fees**: Some mutual fund companies charge account maintenance fees or other administrative fees, such as fees for account transfers, check writing, or wire transfers.

4. **12b-1 Fees**: These fees are charged to cover the costs of marketing and distributing the mutual fund to investors. 12b-1 fees are included in the expense ratio and can be as high as 1% of the fund's assets under management.

5. **Custodial Fees**: If a mutual fund is held in a custodial account, such as an IRA, the custodian may charge a fee for holding the fund.

6. **Other Fees**: Other fees that mutual funds may charge include legal and audit fees, proxy voting expenses, and securities lending fees.

It's essential for you to review a mutual fund's prospectus and other relevant documents to understand all the fees and charges associated with the investment. While some fees, such as management fees and expense ratios, are disclosed prominently, other fees may be buried in the fine print.

Understanding all the fees and expenses can help you to make informed decisions about whether a mutual fund is the right investment for you.

5. IMPACT ON RETURNS

Mutual fund expenses, including sales charges, management fees, expense ratios, and other fees and charges, can have a significant impact on an investor's returns.

Firstly, higher fees can reduce the amount of money available to be invested in the fund, which can lower returns over time. For example, if two funds have the same returns but one has a higher expense ratio, the fund with the higher expenses will result in a lower return for the investor.

Secondly, even small differences in fees can have a significant impact on returns over time due to the compounding effect of investment returns.

For example, if an investor has $10,000 invested in a mutual fund with a 1% expense ratio and earns an average annual return of 8% over 20 years, the investment would grow to approximately $46,610. However, if the same investor invested in a mutual fund with a 0.5% expense ratio, the investment would grow to approximately $53,870. This is a difference of over $7,000 in returns due to the lower expenses of the second fund.

Therefore, it's essential that you consider mutual fund expenses when making investment decisions. While higher fees don't necessarily mean lower returns, you should look for mutual funds with lower expenses to maximize their returns over time.

However, it's important to note that fees shouldn't be the only factor you consider when evaluating mutual funds. Other factors such as the fund's investment strategy, past performance, and risk profile should also be evaluated to determine if the fund is a good fit for your overall investment plan.

11: ASSESSING MUTUAL FUND PERFORMANCE
METRICS AND EVALUATION

O ne of the most important considerations when investing in mutual funds is evaluating their performance. In this chapter, we will explore the different metrics and methods used to evaluate mutual fund performance.

1. NET ASSET VALUE (NAV)

Net Asset Value (NAV) is a measure of the value of a mutual fund's assets minus its liabilities, divided by the number of outstanding shares. The NAV is calculated daily by adding up the current market value of all the securities held by the mutual fund and subtracting any liabilities, such as outstanding debts or expenses.

The NAV is an essential metric for mutual fund investors as it represents the price at which investors can buy or sell shares in the fund. For example, if a mutual fund has a NAV of $20 per share and an investor wants to buy 100 shares, they would need to invest $2,000.

Changes in the NAV reflect changes in the value of the mutual fund's holdings, and therefore, you can use the NAV to track the performance of their investment. If the NAV of a mutual fund increases over time, it suggests that the fund's holdings have appreciated in value, resulting in higher returns for investors. Conversely, if the NAV decreases, it suggests that the fund's holdings have decreased in value, resulting in lower returns.

It's important to note that the NAV only represents the value of a mutual fund's holdings at a specific point in time and doesn't reflect any sales charges, management fees, or other expenses associated with the fund. Therefore, you should also consider other metrics, such as a mutual fund's total return or performance relative to a benchmark index, when evaluating the performance of a mutual fund.

2. TOTAL RETURN

Total return is a measure of a mutual fund's overall performance that takes into account both capital appreciation and income from dividends or interest. Total return represents the total amount an investor earns from a mutual fund over a specific period, including any increase in the fund's NAV and any distributions received from the fund.

The total return can be expressed as a percentage and is calculated as follows:

Total return = (Ending NAV - Beginning NAV + Distributions) / Beginning NAV

For example, if an investor purchased shares in a mutual fund with a NAV of $10 per share and received $1 in dividends over the course of a year, and the fund's NAV increased to $12 per share, the total return for the investor would be 30%.

Total return is an essential metric for evaluating the performance of a mutual fund because it provides a more comprehensive view of the fund's performance than NAV alone. It considers the impact of distributions on an investor's return and provides a measure of the fund's ability to generate income in addition to capital appreciation.

When comparing mutual funds, investors should look at the total return over a specific time frame, such as one, three, or five years, and compare it to the total return of other funds in the same category. Investors should also consider the total return of a mutual fund relative to a benchmark index, such as the S&P 500, to determine whether the fund is outperforming or underperforming the market.

It's important to note that total return doesn't take into account any fees or expenses associated with the mutual fund. Therefore, investors should also consider other metrics, such as expense ratios, sales charges, and management fees, when evaluating the performance of a mutual fund.

3. BENCHMARK COMPARISON

Benchmark comparison is a commonly used approach to assess the performance of mutual funds. A benchmark is a standard used to compare the performance of an investment to a specific market or index.

For example, the S&P 500 is a common benchmark for U.S. large-cap stocks, and the Barclays Aggregate Bond Index is a common benchmark for the U.S. bond market.

By comparing the performance of a mutual fund to a benchmark index, you can determine whether the fund is outperforming or underperforming the market.

For example, if a mutual fund that invests in U.S. large-cap stocks has a total return of 10% over the past year, and the S&P 500 index has a total return of 12% over the same period, the mutual fund has underperformed the benchmark index.

You should compare the performance of a mutual fund to a benchmark that is appropriate for the fund's investment strategy and asset class. For example, a mutual fund that invests in international stocks should be compared to an appropriate international stock index, such as the MSCI EAFE index, rather than a U.S. stock index such as the S&P 500.

Benchmark comparison can help you to identify mutual funds that are generating above-average returns relative to the market or index, and it can also help investors identify mutual funds that are underperforming the market or index.

However, it's important to note that benchmark comparison alone doesn't provide a complete picture of a mutual fund's performance. You should also consider other factors, such as the fund's total return, risk profile, and expense ratio, when evaluating the performance of a mutual fund.

4. RISK-ADJUSTED METRICS

When evaluating the performance of a mutual fund, you should also consider risk-adjusted metrics to determine whether the fund is generating returns that are appropriate for the level of risk taken on by the fund.

Risk-adjusted metrics take into account both the total return of the fund and the level of risk associated with the fund's investments. Two commonly used risk-adjusted metrics are the Sharpe ratio and the Treynor ratio.

The Sharpe ratio measures a mutual fund's excess return per unit of risk. It compares the excess return of the fund (i.e., the return above the risk-free rate) to the fund's volatility, as measured by its standard deviation. A higher Sharpe ratio indicates a better risk-adjusted return.

The Treynor ratio measures a mutual fund's excess return per unit of systematic risk. It compares the excess return of the fund to the fund's beta, which measures the fund's sensitivity to market movements. A higher Treynor ratio indicates a better risk-adjusted return.

Let's imagine that you are looking at two mutual funds that invest in big companies in the US. Fund A has made 12% in profits over the past year, while Fund B has made 15%. You might think Fund B is the better choice because it has higher returns.

But you need to consider more than just the returns. You also need to think about how much the funds charge in fees, and how much risk you are taking. Fund B charges more fees than Fund A, which means you might end up with less money after paying fees.

You also need to think about the risk you're taking. Fund B might have made more money, but it also took on more risk to get those profits. To compare the funds fairly, you can use the Sharpe ratio and Treynor ratio, which take into account both returns and risks.

When you calculate these ratios, you find that Fund A actually has a better risk-adjusted return than Fund B. This means that Fund A made good returns while taking on less risk than Fund B.

So, by looking at all the different factors, you can decide which mutual fund is the better choice for you. It's not just about which fund made the most money, but also about how much it charges in fees and how much risk you are taking.Other risk-adjusted metrics include the Jensen alpha and the Sortino ratio. The Jensen alpha measures a mutual fund's excess return relative to its expected return, as determined by a risk-adjusted model.

A positive Jensen alpha indicates that the fund is generating higher returns than expected, given the level of risk taken on by the fund. The Sortino ratio measures a mutual fund's excess return relative to its downside risk, as measured by the standard deviation of negative returns.

5. EXPENSES

As discussed in the previous chapter, mutual fund expenses can significantly impact an investor's returns.

When evaluating mutual fund performance, it is important to consider the fund's expense ratio and other fees and charges to determine whether the returns generated by the fund are worth the expenses paid.

6. QUALITATIVE ANALYSIS

Qualitative analysis is an approach to evaluating mutual fund performance that involves assessing factors that cannot be measured with numbers. These factors might include the experience and track record of the fund's management team, the fund's investment strategy and philosophy, and the quality of the fund's underlying investments.

One important factor to consider in qualitative analysis is the experience and track record of the fund manager or management team. You might look at the manager's education, certifications, and professional background to get a sense of their expertise in managing investments. You might also examine their track record managing other funds to see how successful they have been in the past.

Another factor to consider is the investment strategy and philosophy of the fund. Does the fund invest in a specific sector, such as technology or healthcare, or does it take a broader approach? Does the fund manager use a passive or active investment strategy, and what is their rationale for this approach? These questions can help you evaluate whether the fund's investment strategy aligns with your own investment goals and risk tolerance.

Finally, it is important to assess the quality of the fund's underlying investments. This might involve looking at the financial statements and reports of the companies the fund invests in, as well as researching industry trends and economic indicators to gain a broader perspective on the fund's investments.

Qualitative analysis is important because it can provide insight into factors that may not be captured by quantitative metrics such as the fund's performance or expense ratio. By considering both quantitative and qualitative factors, investors can gain a more complete understanding of a mutual fund's performance and make more informed investment decisions.

Assessing mutual fund performance is an important part of the investment process. Metrics such as NAV, total return, benchmark comparison, risk-adjusted metrics, and expenses can provide insight into a mutual fund's performance. However, it is important to also consider qualitative factors when evaluating a mutual fund's performance.

By using a combination of quantitative and qualitative analysis, investors can make informed decisions when selecting mutual funds for their portfolio.

As a beginner, this might look intimidating, but as you dig deeper into specific aspects by reading up, you will start to gain greater understanding, which becomes experience as you start your actual investment journey.

12: DIVERSIFICATION
HOW TO SPREAD YOUR INVESTMENTS

Diversification is an important concept in investing, and it refers to spreading your investments across different types of assets or securities. The goal of diversification is to reduce the risk of loss by avoiding concentration in any one particular investment.

1. TYPES OF DIVERSIFICATION

There are several types of diversification that investors can use to spread their investments:

· ASSET ALLOCATION

Asset allocation is a type of diversification that involves spreading investments across different asset classes, such as stocks, bonds, and cash. Asset allocation aims to balance risk and return by investing in a mix of assets that have different risk and return characteristics.

The asset allocation strategy involves determining the optimal mix of different asset classes that aligns with an investor's investment objectives, risk tolerance, and time horizon. The asset allocation decision is based on the principle that different asset classes perform differently under different market conditions.

For example, stocks generally have a higher risk and return profile than bonds, but bonds may provide more stability and income. Cash investments, such as money market funds, are typically considered low-risk but also have low returns.

One of the benefits of asset allocation is that it can help investors manage risk by spreading investments across different asset classes that perform differently under different market conditions.

By investing in a mix of assets, investors can reduce the impact of market volatility and achieve a more stable long-term return.

However, it is important to note that asset allocation does not guarantee a profit or protect against loss. Asset allocation decisions should be based on an investor's unique financial situation, investment objectives, and risk tolerance.

· SECTOR ALLOCATION

Sector allocation is a type of diversification that involves investing in different sectors or industries of the economy. A sector is a group of companies that operate in a specific area of the economy, such as technology, healthcare, energy, or consumer goods.

Sector allocation aims to achieve diversification by investing in a mix of sectors that are expected to perform well over the long term, while avoiding overexposure to any one sector. By investing in multiple sectors, investors can reduce the impact of sector-specific risks, such as changes in government regulations, industry competition, or shifts in consumer demand.

One of the benefits of sector allocation is that it can help investors take advantage of opportunities in specific sectors that are expected to perform well over the long term.

For example, an investor might allocate a higher percentage of their portfolio to the technology sector if they believe that technology companies are likely to experience strong growth in the future.

However, it is important to note that sector allocation does not guarantee a profit or protect against loss. Sector performance can be influenced by a wide range of factors, including global economic conditions, geopolitical events, and market trends.

· GEOGRAPHICAL ALLOCATION

Geographic allocation is a type of diversification strategy that involves investing in different regions or countries around the world. By investing in different geographic regions, investors can balance risk and return by gaining exposure to different economic cycles, political risks, and market conditions.

For example, an investor could invest in a mutual fund that focuses on emerging markets to gain exposure to countries such as China, India, or Brazil, or invest in a fund that focuses on developed markets such as the United States, Europe, or Japan.

One of the benefits of geographic allocation is that it allows investors to access growth opportunities in different regions and economies. For example, emerging markets may offer higher potential growth rates due to their young and growing populations, rapid urbanization, and expanding middle class.

However, it is important to note that geographic allocation also involves additional risks, such as currency risk, political risk, and regulatory risk. Currency risk arises from fluctuations in exchange rates between different currencies, which can impact the returns of international investments.

Political risk arises from changes in government policies or instability in a country's political system, which can impact the economy and the investments in that country. Regulatory risk arises from changes in regulations or laws that can impact the business environment and the investments in that region or country.

Therefore, geographic allocation should be balanced with other types of diversification, such as asset allocation and sector allocation, to manage risk and achieve long-term investment goals. By investing in a mix of regions with different economic cycles, political risks, and market conditions, investors can help achieve their investment goals over the long term while managing risk.

· INDIVIDUAL SECURITY SELECTION

Individual security selection is a type of diversification that involves selecting and investing in individual stocks, bonds, or other securities. This approach involves choosing specific investments based on an analysis of their fundamental characteristics, such as earnings, cash flow, and financial health, rather than relying on diversification through mutual funds or other pooled investments.

Investing in individual securities can provide a level of customization and control over a portfolio that is not available through mutual funds or other pooled investments. For example, an investor may choose to invest in individual securities that align with their personal values or beliefs, or they may have a particular expertise in a certain industry or sector and want to invest in specific companies in that area.

However, individual security selection also comes with a higher level of risk than investing in diversified funds. By investing in a single security, an investor is exposed to the risk of that particular security performing poorly or experiencing significant losses. This risk can be mitigated through thorough research and analysis of individual securities, as well as through proper diversification across different sectors and asset classes.

2. BENEFITS OF DIVERSIFICATION

Diversification offers several benefits to investors, including:

- **Reducing Risk:** By spreading investments across different types of assets or securities, investors can reduce the risk of loss associated with any one particular investment.

- **Improving Returns:** Diversification can also help improve returns by allowing investors to capture gains in different asset classes or sectors.

- **Providing Flexibility:** Diversification provides investors with flexibility to adjust their portfolios based on changing market conditions.

3. RISKS OF DIVERSIFICATION

While diversification can help reduce overall risk, it is important to note that it does not eliminate risk entirely. Some risks of diversification include:

- **Over-Diversification:** Investing in too many securities can dilute returns and make it difficult to track performance.

- **Correlation Risk:** Some assets may be highly correlated with each other, meaning they tend to move in the same direction. This can reduce the benefits of diversification.

- **Opportunity Cost:** By spreading investments across multiple assets or securities, investors may miss out on potential gains from concentrated positions.

4. BUILDING A DIVERSIFIED PORTFOLIO

To build a diversified portfolio, investors should consider their investment goals, risk tolerance, and time horizon. They should also consider diversification across asset classes, sectors, and regions. Finally, they should regularly monitor and adjust their portfolio to ensure it remains diversified and aligned with their investment objectives.

***

Diversification is an essential component of investing and can help reduce risk while improving returns. By spreading investments across different asset classes, sectors, and regions, you can create a diversified portfolio that aligns with your investment goals and risk tolerance.

However, it is important to note that diversification does not eliminate risk entirely, and you should regularly monitor and adjust your portfolio to ensure they remain diversified and aligned with your investment objectives.

13: ASSET ALLOCATION
CREATING A BALANCED PORTFOLIO

Asset allocation is a crucial element of investment management. It refers to the process of dividing an investment portfolio among different asset categories, such as stocks, bonds, and cash, based on an your goals, risk tolerance, and investment horizon.

1. IMPORTANCE OF ASSET ALLOCATION

Asset allocation is important because it has a significant impact on portfolio performance. Research has shown that asset allocation is responsible for the majority of a portfolio's return, rather than individual security selection or market timing.

2. DETERMINING ASSET ALLOCATION

When determining asset allocation, investors should consider their investment objectives, risk tolerance, and investment horizon. They should also consider their current financial situation, including income, expenses, and existing assets and liabilities.

3. ASSET CLASSES

There are several different asset classes that investors can consider when creating a balanced portfolio, including:

- **Equities:** Stocks represent ownership in a company and can provide growth potential and income through dividends. However, they are typically more volatile and risky than other asset classes.

- **Fixed income:** Bonds represent debt obligations issued by companies or governments and provide income through interest payments. They are typically less risky than equities but may provide lower returns.

- **Cash and cash equivalents:** These are short-term investments, such as savings accounts and money market funds, that provide liquidity and stability.

- **Alternative investments:** These include assets such as real estate, commodities, and hedge funds. They can provide diversification and potential for higher returns but may also be more complex and risky.

4. BALANCING ASSET ALLOCATION

Once you have determined your desired asset allocation, you must balance their portfolio to ensure it aligns with your goals and risk tolerance. This involves selecting specific investments within each asset class, such as individual stocks or bonds, and diversifying across different sectors and regions.

5. REBALANCING ASSET ALLOCATION

Finally, regularly monitor and rebalance your portfolios to ensure they remain aligned with your investment objectives. Rebalancing involves selling or buying assets to maintain the desired asset allocation. This helps ensure that the portfolio remains balanced and aligned with the your goals and risk tolerance.

***

Asset allocation is a crucial component of creating a balanced investment portfolio. By diversifying across different asset classes, you can reduce risk and improve returns.

When determining asset allocation, consider your investment goals, risk tolerance, and investment horizon. Also regularly monitor and rebalance your portfolios to ensure they remain aligned with your investment objectives.

14: BUILDING A MUTUAL FUND PORTFOLIO
STRATEGIES AND CONSIDERATIONS

Building a mutual fund portfolio requires careful consideration of various factors, such as investment goals, risk tolerance, and time horizon. In this chapter, we will discuss some strategies and considerations to keep in mind when building a mutual fund portfolio.

1. DEFINE INVESTMENT GOALS

Before selecting any mutual fund, you must define your investment goals. This involves answering questions like, "What am I investing for?" and "When will I need the money?"

Based on these answers, you can identify the types of mutual funds that align with your financial goals.

2. DETERMINE RISK TOLERANCE

You must also determine your risk tolerance. This involves assessing how much risk you are willing to take on in pursuit of your investment goals. Based on your risk tolerance, you can select mutual funds that align with your preferences.

3. CONSIDER TIME HORIZON

You must also consider your time horizon. This involves assessing how long you have until you need the money you are investing. Based on your time horizon, you can select mutual funds with an appropriate investment strategy.

4. DIVERSIFY YOUR PORTFOLIO

Diversification is key to building a successful mutual fund portfolio. This involves selecting mutual funds that invest in different asset classes, such as stocks, bonds, and cash. By diversifying, you can reduce your overall risk and improve your returns.

5. ALLOCATE ASSETS ACROSS SECTORS

In addition to diversifying across asset classes, you should also consider diversifying across sectors. For example, you might choose to allocate your equity investments across different sectors, such as technology, healthcare, and consumer goods. This helps to further reduce risk and improve returns.

6. SELECT MUTUAL FUNDS WITH LOW EXPENSES

Expense ratios can eat into your returns over time. To minimize the impact of expenses, you should select mutual funds with low expense ratios.

7. CONSIDER PAST PERFORMANCE

While past performance is not a guarantee of future returns, it can be a helpful indicator of a mutual fund's investment strategy and success. You should consider a mutual fund's past performance when selecting mutual funds to include in your portfolio.

8. REGULARLY MONITOR AND ADJUST YOUR PORTFOLIO

Finally, regularly monitor your mutual fund portfolio and adjust it as needed. This involves rebalancing the portfolio to maintain an appropriate asset allocation and making changes to the portfolio as investment goals or market conditions change.

***

Building a mutual fund portfolio requires careful consideration of investment goals, risk tolerance, time horizon, and diversification.

By following these strategies and considerations, you can build a well-diversified portfolio of mutual funds that aligns with your investment goals and risk preferences. Regularly monitoring and adjusting the portfolio is also important to ensure it remains aligned with your goals and changing market conditions.

15: DETERMINING YOUR INVESTMENT GOALS AND RISK TOLERANCE

I nvesting in mutual funds can help you build wealth over the long term. However, before you start investing, it is important to determine your investment goals and risk tolerance. This will help you make informed investment decisions and create a portfolio that aligns with your financial goals.

INVESTMENT GOALS

Your investment goals should be specific, measurable, achievable, relevant, and time-bound (SMART). Ask yourself the following questions to help determine your investment goals:

1. What are you investing for?

2. How much money do you want to accumulate?

3. When do you need the money?

4. What is your investment time horizon?

5. What is your current financial situation?

6. What is your risk tolerance?

Once you have answers to these questions, you can create specific investment goals.

For example, your investment goal may be to save $500,000 for retirement in 30 years. This goal is specific, measurable, achievable, relevant, and time-bound.

RISK TOLERANCE

Risk tolerance is the level of risk you are willing to take when investing. Your risk tolerance is influenced by your investment goals, age, income, and financial situation. It is important to understand your risk tolerance because it affects the types of mutual funds you should invest in.

Conservative investors have a low tolerance for risk and prefer investments that offer stable returns. They are generally risk-averse and prefer fixed-income investments such as bond funds or money market funds.

Moderate investors have a moderate tolerance for risk and prefer a balance of stability and growth. They may invest in a combination of equity funds and fixed-income funds.

Aggressive investors have a high tolerance for risk and are willing to invest in investments that offer high growth potential but also come with higher risk. They may invest in a combination of equity funds, alternative investment funds, and other high-risk investments.

It is important to note that risk tolerance is not a fixed characteristic and may change over time. As your investment goals and financial situation change, your risk tolerance may also change.

***

Determining your investment goals and risk tolerance is a critical first step to building a successful investment portfolio. Your investment goals should be specific, measurable, achievable, relevant, and time-bound.

Your risk tolerance is influenced by your investment goals, age, income, and financial situation. By understanding your investment goals and risk tolerance, you can create a portfolio that aligns with your long-term financial objectives.

16: OPENING A BROKERAGE ACCOUNT

Once you have determined your investment goals and risk tolerance, the next step is to open a brokerage account. A brokerage account is a type of investment account that allows you to buy and sell securities such as mutual funds, stocks, and bonds. Here are the steps to opening a brokerage account:

1: RESEARCH BROKERAGES

When researching brokerages, it's important to consider several factors to help you find the right one for your investment needs.

Here are some key factors to consider:

a. **Fees**: Brokerages may charge fees for different services, such as account maintenance, trading fees, and transaction fees. Make sure to compare fees across different brokerages and consider how they will impact your investment returns.

b. **Investment Options**: Different brokerages offer different investment options, including different types of mutual funds, stocks, bonds, and other securities. Make sure to choose a brokerage that offers the types of investments you are interested in.

c. **Customer Service**: Consider the level of customer service provided by each brokerage. You want to choose a brokerage that is responsive to your needs and provides the support you need when making investment decisions.

d. **User Interface**: The user interface of the brokerage platform can have a significant impact on your investing experience. Make sure to choose a brokerage with a user-friendly platform that you are comfortable using.

e. **Account Minimums**: Some brokerages require a minimum account balance to open an account. Make sure to choose a brokerage that has a minimum account balance that you can afford.

f. **Regulatory Compliance**: Make sure the brokerage you choose is regulated by a reputable regulatory agency, such as the Securities and Exchange Commission (SEC) in the United States. This ensures that the brokerage is subject to oversight and that your investments are protected.

g. **Reputation**: Research the reputation of the brokerage to ensure that it has a good track record and is trusted by investors. You can do this by reading reviews and checking the brokerage's regulatory history.

h. **Additional Services**: Some brokerages offer additional services such as financial planning, research tools, and educational resources. Consider whether these services are important to you and if they are worth paying extra for.

By considering these factors, you can make an informed decision when choosing a brokerage to open your mutual fund investment account. It's important to take your time to research different brokerages and choose one that aligns with your investment goals and preferences.

2: CHOOSE A BROKERAGE

Once you have researched different brokerages, choose one that aligns with your investment goals and preferences.

Getting recommendations from investment savvy friends, family or colleagues is also helpful.

3: FILL OUT AN APPLICATION

Opening a brokerage account typically involves filling out an application form with a financial institution that offers brokerage services. A brokerage account allows you to invest in a range of financial products, including stocks, bonds, mutual funds, and exchange-traded funds (ETFs).

The application process for opening a brokerage account typically involves providing personal information such as your name, address, date of birth, and social security number.

You may also be required to provide information about your employment status, income, and investment objectives. Some brokerage firms may also require you to provide additional documentation, such as a copy of your driver's license or passport.

In addition to the application form, you may also need to sign various documents, including a customer agreement, risk disclosure statements, and a privacy policy. These documents outline the terms and conditions of the brokerage account, as well as the risks associated with investing in the financial markets.

It is important to carefully review all documents before signing them and to ask any questions you may have about the account or the investment products available.

Once your application is approved and your account is set up, you can begin to deposit funds into the account and start investing in the financial markets.

4: FUND YOUR ACCOUNT

After your brokerage account application is approved and your account is set up, the next step is to fund your account. Funding your brokerage account means transferring money into the account, so you can start buying and selling securities.

There are several ways to fund your brokerage account, depending on the brokerage firm you use. Some common methods include:

a. **Electronic Funds Transfer (EFT) or Automated Clearing House (ACH)**: You can transfer money from your bank account to your brokerage account using an EFT or ACH transfer. This is a secure and convenient way to fund your account.

b. **Wire transfer**: You can wire funds directly from your bank to your brokerage account. This method is usually faster than EFT or ACH transfer but may have higher fees.

c. **Check**: You can also deposit a check into your brokerage account. However, it may take longer for the funds to clear and become available for trading.

It is important to note that brokerage firms may have different requirements for minimum account balances and may charge fees for certain types of transactions or account maintenance. Make sure to review your brokerage firm's fee schedule before funding your account.

Once your account is funded, you can start buying and selling securities. It is important to have a solid investment strategy in place and to be aware of the risks involved in investing in the financial markets. It is also important to keep track of your account balance and to regularly review your investment portfolio to ensure it aligns with your investment objectives.

***

Opening a brokerage account is a critical step to investing in mutual funds. By researching different brokerages and choosing one that aligns with your investment goals and preferences, you can open an account and start investing. Remember to choose mutual funds that align with your investment goals and risk tolerance and to monitor your investments regularly to ensure they are performing as expected.

17: CHOOSING YOUR MUTUAL FUNDS

C hoosing the right mutual funds to invest in is crucial to building a successful investment portfolio. Mutual funds are a popular investment option because they offer diversification and professional management, but with so many options available, it can be overwhelming to choose the right ones.

Here are some key factors to consider when choosing your mutual funds:

1. INVESTMENT OBJECTIVES

The first step in choosing mutual funds is to determine your investment objectives. Are you looking for growth, income, or a combination of both? Different mutual funds have different investment objectives, so it is important to choose funds that align with your goals.

2. RISK TOLERANCE

Mutual funds vary in terms of risk, with some funds investing in more volatile assets than others. It is important to consider your risk tolerance and choose funds that align with your comfort level.

3. FUND PERFORMANCE

Past performance is not a guarantee of future results, but it is still an important factor to consider when choosing mutual funds. Look for funds that have a consistent track record of outperforming their benchmark index over multiple time periods.

4. EXPENSE RATIO

Mutual funds charge fees for management and operating expenses, which are reflected in the fund's expense ratio. Lower expense ratios mean more of your investment goes towards actual investment returns, so it is important to choose funds with low expense ratios.

5. FUND MANAGER

The fund manager plays a crucial role in the success of the mutual fund. Look for funds with experienced and reputable fund managers with a strong track record of performance.

6. DIVERSIFICATION

Diversification is important to reduce risk and maximize returns. Look for mutual funds that invest in a range of asset classes, sectors, and geographies to achieve a diversified portfolio.

7. FUND SIZE

While larger funds may offer economies of scale and better liquidity, smaller funds may be more nimble and able to take advantage of investment opportunities. Consider the size of the mutual fund when making your selection.

8. INVESTMENT STYLE

Mutual funds may follow different investment styles, such as value or growth investing. Choose funds that align with your investment style and goals.

9. TAX EFFICIENCY

Mutual funds may generate taxable income or capital gains, which can impact your after-tax returns. Look for funds with a history of tax-efficient investing.

**

Choosing the right mutual funds requires careful consideration of your investment objectives, risk tolerance, past performance, expense ratio, fund manager, diversification, fund size, investment style, and tax efficiency. It is important to do your research and choose funds that align with your goals and values to build a successful investment portfolio.

18: DECIDING HOW MUCH TO INVEST

One of the most important decisions you will make when investing in mutual funds is how much to invest. The amount you invest will depend on several factors, including your financial goals, current financial situation, and risk tolerance.

Here are some factors to consider when deciding how much to invest in mutual funds:

1. FINANCIAL GOALS

The first step in determining how much to invest is to consider your financial goals. Are you investing for short-term goals, such as a down payment on a home, or for long-term goals, such as retirement? Your investment goals will help you determine how much you need to invest and for how long.

2. CURRENT FINANCIAL SITUATION

Your current financial situation will also play a role in how much you can invest. Consider your income, expenses, debt, and other financial obligations when deciding how much to invest.

3. RISK TOLERANCE

Your risk tolerance will impact the amount you should invest. If you have a low risk tolerance, you may want to invest a smaller amount and choose more conservative mutual funds. If you have a higher risk tolerance, you may be comfortable investing a larger amount and choosing more aggressive mutual funds.

4. ASSET ALLOCATION

Your asset allocation strategy will also impact how much you should invest. If you plan to invest in a range of asset classes, such as stocks, bonds, and cash, you may need to allocate a larger amount to mutual funds to achieve a diversified portfolio.

5. COST OF LIVING

The cost of living in your area may impact how much you can invest. If you live in a high-cost area, you may need to allocate more of your income to living expenses, which may impact how much you can invest.

6. EMERGENCY FUND

It is important to have an emergency fund in place before investing in mutual funds. Consider setting aside three to six months' worth of living expenses in a savings account before investing in mutual funds.

Determining how much to invest in mutual funds requires careful consideration of your financial goals, current financial situation, risk tolerance, asset allocation, cost of living, and emergency fund.

It is important to have a clear understanding of your financial situation and goals before investing and to make sure you have an emergency fund in place, and start out by only investing money that you can afford to lose.

19: PLACING YOUR ORDER

Once you have chosen the mutual funds you want to invest in and have determined how much you want to invest, the next step is to place your order. Placing your order involves submitting your investment request to your brokerage or mutual fund company.

Here are the steps to follow when placing your order:

1. CONTACT YOUR BROKERAGE OR MUTUAL FUND COMPANY

The first step is to contact your brokerage or mutual fund company to place your order. You can do this through their website, mobile app, or by phone.

2. CHOOSE YOUR INVESTMENT TYPE

You will need to choose the type of investment you want to make, such as a one-time investment or setting up a recurring investment plan.

3. SELECT YOUR MUTUAL FUNDS

Choose the mutual funds you want to invest in and the amount you want to invest in each fund. You may also need to provide your account information, such as your account number and routing number.

4. VERIFY YOUR ORDER DETAILS

Before submitting your order to invest in mutual funds, it is crucial to verify all the details to ensure that you are investing in the right mutual funds and the right amount. Here are some specific details to verify:

a. **Mutual Fund Name**: Verify that the mutual fund name you have selected is the correct one. Check the ticker symbol and the name to make sure they match with your intended investment.

b. **Investment Amount**: Double-check the amount you want to invest in each mutual fund. Make sure that it is within your budget and matches your investment goals.

c. **Fees and Expenses**: Take note of any fees and expenses associated with the mutual fund investment. Ensure that you understand the impact of the fees on your investment returns.

d. **Account Information**: Confirm that your account information, such as your account number and routing number, are correct. Any errors in your account information can lead to delays in processing your investment order.

e. **Investment Type**: Ensure that you have selected the right investment type. For example, if you want to make a one-time investment, make sure that you have not inadvertently signed up for a recurring investment plan.

f. **Risk Profile**: Review the risk profile of the mutual funds you have chosen. Make sure that the funds align with your investment goals and risk tolerance.

g. **Order Details**: Check that the order details, such as the investment date, are accurate.

By verifying all the order details, you can avoid any mistakes or errors that may negatively impact your investment returns. It is important to take the time to carefully review your order before submitting it to ensure that you are investing in the right mutual funds and the right amount.

5. **SUBMIT YOUR ORDER**

Once you have verified all the details, you can submit your order. Your brokerage or mutual fund company will process your order and invest your funds in the selected mutual funds.

***

Placing your order to invest in mutual funds involves contacting your brokerage or mutual fund company, choosing your investment type, selecting your mutual funds, verifying your order details, submitting your order, and monitoring your investments. It is important to make sure you understand the process and to monitor your investments regularly to ensure they are performing as expected.

20: MONITORING YOUR INVESTMENTS

Investing in mutual funds is a long-term strategy that requires patience and consistency. Once you have invested your money in mutual funds, it is important to monitor your investments regularly to ensure they are performing as expected and to make any necessary adjustments.

Here are some tips for monitoring your mutual fund investments:

1. KEEP TRACK OF YOUR INVESTMENT PERFORMANCE

Check your mutual fund investment performance regularly, either through your brokerage or mutual fund company's website or by reviewing your statements. Monitor the fund's performance over different time frames, such as one year, three years, five years, and ten years, to see how the fund is performing over time.

2. UNDERSTAND THE FEES AND EXPENSES

Review the fees and expenses associated with your mutual fund investments. Make sure you understand how the fees are impacting your investment returns and if there are any cheaper alternatives available.

3. REBALANCE YOUR PORTFOLIO

Over time, your mutual fund investments may become unbalanced due to market fluctuations or changes in your investment goals. Review your portfolio regularly and consider rebalancing it by selling some funds and investing in others.

4. STAY INFORMED

Keep up-to-date with the news and trends in the market that may impact your mutual fund investments. Follow financial news outlets and consult with a financial advisor to stay informed about potential risks or opportunities.

5. REVIEW YOUR INVESTMENT GOALS

Review your investment goals periodically to ensure that your mutual fund investments align with them. If your investment goals have changed, consider adjusting your mutual fund portfolio accordingly.

6. BE PATIENT

Investing in mutual funds is a long-term strategy that requires patience and consistency. Avoid making hasty decisions based on short-term market fluctuations and focus on your long-term investment goals.

By monitoring your mutual fund investments regularly, you can ensure that you are on track to meet your investment goals and make any necessary adjustments. It is important to stay informed and be patient, as investing in mutual funds is a long-term strategy that requires time and discipline.

21: STAYING COMMITTED TO YOUR INVESTMENT PLAN

Investing in mutual funds can be a smart way to build long-term wealth, but it's important to remember that it's a marathon, not a sprint. Staying committed to your investment plan can be challenging, but it's essential if you want to achieve your financial goals. Here are some tips to help you stay on track:

1. REMEMBER YOUR GOALS

It's easy to get caught up in day-to-day market fluctuations and lose sight of your long-term investment goals. Regularly remind yourself of why you started investing in the first place, and the financial goals you hope to achieve.

2. STICK TO YOUR PLAN

When you create an investment plan, you should have a clear idea of your risk tolerance, asset allocation, and time horizon. It's important to stick to this plan even when market conditions are turbulent. Resist the temptation to make emotional decisions based on short-term fluctuations and focus on your long-term goals.

3. REBALANCE YOUR PORTFOLIO

Over time, your investment portfolio may become unbalanced as certain assets outperform others. Rebalancing your portfolio involves selling some of your winners and reinvesting the proceeds into underperforming assets. This ensures that your portfolio stays aligned with your long-term goals and risk tolerance.

4. INVEST REGULARLY

Investing regularly, even during market downturns, can help you take advantage of dollar-cost averaging. This means that you're buying more shares when prices are low, which can lead to higher returns over the long-term. Set up automatic investments into your mutual funds to ensure that you're investing consistently.

5. REVIEW YOUR PLAN ANNUALLY

Your financial situation, goals, and risk tolerance may change over time. It's important to review your investment plan annually and make any necessary adjustments. This can help ensure that your portfolio stays aligned with your long-term goals.

6. SEEK PROFESSIONAL HELP

If you're struggling to stay committed to your investment plan, consider seeking professional help from a financial advisor. They can help you create a customized investment plan based on your financial situation and goals, and provide guidance on how to stay on track.

Staying committed to your investment plan can be challenging, but it's essential if you want to achieve your long-term financial goals. Remember to stay focused on your goals, stick to your plan, and seek professional help when needed. With a little discipline and patience, you can build long-term wealth through smart investing in mutual funds.

22. RISKS AND CHALLENGES IN MUTUAL FUND INVESTING

Investing in mutual funds can provide many benefits, but it's important to understand the risks and challenges involved. In this chapter, we will discuss some of the key risks and challenges associated with mutual fund investing.

MARKET RISK

One of the primary risks of investing in mutual funds is market risk. The value of mutual fund investments can be impacted by changes in the stock market, interest rates, and other economic factors. Market fluctuations can cause the value of your mutual fund holdings to increase or decrease, and it's important to be prepared for these fluctuations.

MANAGER RISK

Another risk associated with mutual funds is manager risk. Mutual funds are managed by investment professionals who make decisions about which securities to buy and sell. If the fund manager makes poor investment decisions or if the manager leaves the fund, it can have a negative impact on the fund's performance.

EXPENSE RATIO

Mutual funds also come with expenses that can impact your returns. The expense ratio includes the fees and expenses charged by the mutual fund company for managing the fund. It's important to consider the expense ratio when choosing mutual funds and to look for funds with lower expenses to help maximize your returns.

CONCENTRATION RISK

Investing in a single mutual fund or a group of funds with similar investments can lead to concentration risk. If the mutual fund is heavily invested in a particular sector or region, it can be vulnerable to market fluctuations in that area. Diversifying your portfolio across multiple mutual funds can help mitigate this risk.

LIQUIDITY RISK

Mutual funds can also have liquidity risk. This means that it may be difficult to sell your shares of the fund quickly or at a fair price. This can occur when the fund invests in securities that are illiquid or difficult to sell.

CHALLENGES WITH FUND SELECTION

Selecting the right mutual funds can also be a challenge. With thousands of mutual funds to choose from, it can be difficult to identify the best options for your investment goals and risk tolerance. It's important to research and compare different mutual funds before making a decision.

While mutual fund investing can offer many benefits, it's important to understand the risks and challenges involved. Market risk, manager risk, expense ratios, concentration risk, liquidity risk, and challenges with fund selection are all important factors to consider when investing in mutual funds.

By being aware of these risks and challenges and taking steps to mitigate them, you can help build a diversified portfolio that aligns with your investment objectives.

23: TAXATION OF MUTUAL FUNDS
IMPLICATIONS AND STRATEGIES

While mutual funds can be an excellent investment vehicle, it is essential to understand the tax implications of investing in them. In this chapter, we will discuss the taxation of mutual funds and strategies to minimize your tax liability.

CAPITAL GAINS AND DIVIDEND TAXES

When you invest in mutual funds, you will be subject to taxes on capital gains and dividends. Capital gains are the profits that mutual funds earn when they sell securities at a higher price than they paid for them. Dividends are payments made to shareholders by the mutual fund companies, typically generated from the dividends and interest earned by the underlying securities.

SHORT-TERM AND LONG-TERM CAPITAL GAINS

Capital gains are classified as either short-term or long-term. If a mutual fund sells a security within one year of purchase, the gain is considered short-term. Short-term capital gains are taxed at the same rate as your regular income, which can be as high as 37%. On the other hand, long-term capital gains are generated when a mutual fund sells a security after holding it for more than a year. Long-term capital gains are taxed at lower rates, ranging from 0% to 20% depending on your income.

DIVIDEND TAXES

Dividends paid out by mutual funds are subject to income tax.

However, qualified dividends are taxed at the lower long-term capital gains tax rates, while non-qualified dividends are taxed at the higher ordinary income tax rates.

TAX-EFFICIENT STRATEGIES

There are several strategies you can employ to minimize your tax liability when investing in mutual funds:

1. **Invest In Tax-Efficient Funds**: Certain mutual funds are designed to minimize taxes, such as index funds or exchange-traded funds (ETFs) that track a specific index.

2. **Hold Funds For The Long Term**: Holding mutual funds for more than a year can reduce your tax liability, as you will be subject to the lower long-term capital gains tax rate.

3. **Tax-Loss Harvesting**: This strategy involves selling losing investments to offset gains from other investments, thus reducing your tax liability. Be aware that there are specific rules and restrictions surrounding this strategy, and it's best to consult with a tax professional before implementing it.

4. **Consider Tax-Managed Funds**: Tax-managed mutual funds are specifically designed to minimize taxes. They do this by actively managing the fund's portfolio to minimize capital gains and maximize tax efficiency.

5. **Maximize Tax-Sheltered Accounts**: Investing in mutual funds within tax-sheltered accounts such as Individual Retirement Accounts (IRAs) or 401(k)s can help minimize your tax liability. Contributions to these accounts are tax-deductible or made with pre-tax dollars, and any capital gains and dividends earned within the account are not subject to taxes until withdrawal.

Investing in mutual funds can be a lucrative way to grow your wealth, but it's crucial to consider the tax implications of these investments. Understanding the taxation of mutual funds and implementing tax-efficient strategies can help minimize your tax liability and maximize your investment returns. It's essential to consult with a tax professional to determine the best tax strategy for your individual financial situation.

24: BUILDING WEALTH WITH MUTUAL FUNDS

Mutual funds can be an excellent tool for building long-term wealth. In this chapter, we will discuss how to use mutual funds to build your investment portfolio and achieve your financial goals.

1. START EARLY AND INVEST CONSISTENTLY

One of the most important keys to building wealth with mutual funds is to start early and invest consistently. By starting early, you give your investments more time to grow, and by investing consistently, you take advantage of the power of compounding.

2. DIVERSIFY YOUR PORTFOLIO

Diversification is essential in investing because it helps reduce risk. Investing in mutual funds allows you to diversify your portfolio by spreading your investment across a variety of assets like stocks, bonds, and other securities.

3. CHOOSE FUNDS WITH A LONG-TERM TRACK RECORD OF SUCCESS

When selecting mutual funds, it is important to choose funds with a long-term track record of success. Look for funds that have consistently outperformed their benchmark over a period of several years.

4. CONSIDER INDEX FUNDS

Index funds are an excellent choice for investors who want

to passively invest in the stock market. These funds track a specific index, such as the S&P 500, and offer low fees and broad diversification.

5. MONITOR YOUR PORTFOLIO REGULARLY

Regularly monitoring your portfolio is essential to ensure that your investments remain in line with your financial goals. Rebalance your portfolio periodically to maintain the appropriate level of diversification and risk.

6. STAY THE COURSE DURING MARKET DOWNTURNS

Market downturns can be challenging, but they are a normal part of investing. Staying the course during these downturns is essential to achieving long-term wealth-building goals.

Keep in mind that the market has historically recovered from downturns, and selling during a downturn can result in missing out on potential gains.

By following these tips, you can use mutual funds to build long-term wealth and achieve your financial goals. Remember, investing takes time and patience, but the rewards can be significant.

25: COMMON INVESTOR MISTAKES

Investing in mutual funds can be a great way to grow your wealth over the long term. However, there are some common mistakes that investors make that can impact their returns. In this chapter, we will discuss some of the most common investor mistakes and how to avoid them.

1. CHASING PERFORMANCE

Many investors make the mistake of investing in mutual funds that have recently outperformed the market. This approach, known as chasing performance, can be dangerous.

Funds that have performed well in the past may not necessarily continue to do so in the future. It is essential to focus on the fund's underlying investment strategy, long-term performance, and risk profile before making an investment decision.

2. FAILING TO DIVERSIFY

Diversification is one of the key principles of successful investing. By spreading your investments across a range of assets, you can reduce your exposure to risk.

Many investors make the mistake of investing in just one or two mutual funds, rather than diversifying their portfolio. It is important to invest in a mix of asset classes, sectors, and geographic regions to minimize risk.

3. TIMING THE MARKET

Many investors try to time the market by buying and selling mutual funds based on market trends or predictions.

This approach is risky and can lead to significant losses. It is almost impossible to predict short-term market movements, and attempting to time the market can cause investors to miss out on long-term gains.

4. IGNORING FEES

Mutual funds charge fees for management, administration, and other expenses. These fees can significantly impact your returns over the long term. Many investors make the mistake of ignoring these fees or failing to understand how they impact their returns.

It is important to read the fund's prospectus carefully to understand the fees you will be charged and to compare fees across different mutual funds.

5. OVERREACTING TO MARKET VOLATILITY

The stock market is volatile, and it is not uncommon for mutual fund prices to fluctuate significantly over short periods. Many investors make the mistake of overreacting to market volatility and selling their mutual fund holdings during a downturn. This knee-jerk reaction can cause investors to miss out on long-term gains.

Avoiding these common investor mistakes can help you maximize your returns when investing in mutual funds. By focusing on long-term performance, diversifying your portfolio, ignoring short-term market movements, paying attention to fees, and staying the course during market downturns, you can build a successful investment portfolio.

26: CONCLUSION AND NEXT STEPS

Congratulations on completing Investing in Mutual Funds 101: A Beginner's Guide to Building Wealth through Smart Investing. By now, you should have a better understanding of mutual funds, how they work, and the benefits of investing in them.

As a beginner investor, it's essential to continue educating yourself on personal finance and investing.

Here are some next steps to consider:

1. **Develop a long-term investment strategy**: Consider your financial goals, risk tolerance, and time horizon to develop an investment plan that aligns with your objectives.

2. **Research mutual funds**: Use the knowledge you've gained to research and evaluate mutual funds that fit your investment strategy. Look for funds with a solid track record of performance, low fees, and experienced management.

3. **Diversify your portfolio**: Diversification is key to mitigating risk in your portfolio. Consider investing in a mix of asset classes, including stocks, bonds, and real estate investment trusts (REITs).

4. **Monitor your investments**: Stay up-to-date on your mutual fund investments' performance and monitor them regularly to ensure they align with your investment strategy.

Remember, investing is a long-term strategy that requires patience and discipline. Don't let short-term market fluctuations or emotional reactions drive your investment decisions.

Thank you for reading Investing in Mutual Funds 101: A Beginner's Guide to Building Wealth Through Smart Investing.

We hope this guide has been helpful in your journey to building long-term wealth through smart investing.

ABOUT THE AUTHOR

Usiere Uko

Usiere Uko is a writer, speaker and business and finance coach. Aside from running other businesses, he is involved in helping entrepreneurs grow their businesses and attain their potential through a faith-based business academy and empowerment programs.

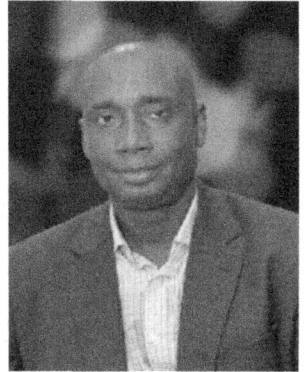

Originally trained as a mechanical engineer with extensive experience in the oil industry spanning design, construction, project management and organisational capability, his passion has been to educate people to achieve their fullest potential and live fully through acquiring skills (especially financial skills) to enable them to achieve freedom in other areas of their lives as an integrated whole.

Among the publications he has written for includes Punch (AM Business) and Daily Trust (SME Business) Newspapers, Leadership & Lifestyle and Today's Lifeline magazines.

Usiere lives is happily married with a lovely son and daughter.

BOOKS BY THIS AUTHOR

Practical Steps To Financial Freedom And Independence: Money Management Skills For Beginners

A Simple Guide To Investing In The Money Market: How To Start Making Your Money Work Hard For You

Before You Trade Forex: Things You Need To Know If You Desire To Start Trading Forex Profitably

Before You Invest In Cryptocurrency: A Simple Guide To Understanding The Cryptocurrency Market

101 Common Money Mistakes To Avoid: And How To Fix Them. Book 1: Expenses. Money Management, Making Your Budget Work

How To Invest In Bonds: A Beginner's Guide To Bonds Investment

How To Invest In Treasury Bills: A Beginner's Guide To Treasury Bonds Investing

How To Avoid Living Under Financial Pressure: A Simple Guide To Getting Back Control Of Your Finances

Financial Independence For Employees: Making Your Job A Stepping Stone To Exiting The Rat Race And Living Your Dreams

Managing Your Money Post Covid: Financial Management Skills For An Era Of High Inflation And Market Disruption

Retire On Your Own Terms: A Simple Guide To Financially Literate Retirement Planning

Your Ultimate Money Makeover: Manage Your Money Better, Take Control Of Your Finances And Your Life

Teaching Kids Money 101: Simple Parenting Strategies For Raising Financially Literate Kids From Toddler To Teen Years And Beyond

Uncle Ben's Money Lessons: Book I: Do You Want To Work For Money? A Vacation Story With An Adventure Into The World Of Money

Nft Investing 101: A Beginner's Guide To Collectible Digital Assets

Stock Market Investing 101: A Practical Beginners Guide To Online And Offline Stock Trading

Investing In Etfs 101: A Beginner's Guide For Building Wealth With Exchange-Traded Funds

Made in the USA
Las Vegas, NV
01 May 2024

89377696R00069